Christmas

Recipes & Crafts

Christmas
Recipes & Crafts

FOR THE PERFECT
HOMEMADE CHRISTMAS

This edition published by Parragon Books Ltd in 2015 and distributed by

Parragon Inc.
440 Park Avenue South, 13th Floor
New York, NY 10016
www.parragon.com/lovefood

LOVE FOOD is an imprint of Parragon Books Ltd

ISBN 978-1-4723-9260-2

Printed in China

Project managed by Annabel King
Introduction by Robin Donovan
New crafts by Clare Lloyd
New recipe photography by Mike Cooper
New craft and incidental photography by Henry Sparrow
Cover photography by Ian Garlick
Edited by Fiona Biggs

Title font: Saint Agnes © Great Lakes Lettering

Notes for the Reader

This book uses standard kitchen measuring spoons and cups. All spoon and cup
measurements are level unless otherwise indicated. Unless otherwise stated, milk is assumed
to be whole, eggs are large, individual vegetables are medium, and pepper is freshly ground
black pepper. Unless otherwise stated, all root vegetables should be peeled prior to using.

The times given are only an approximate guide. Preparation times differ according to the
techniques used by different people and the cooking times may also vary from those given.

For best results, use a food thermometer when cooking meat. Check the latest government
guidelines for current advice.

Contents

Introduction

There's no denying it. Christmas is a truly magical time of year. There's the crisp, cool bite of winter air, the smell of pine needles, twinkling lights, and, if you're lucky, even a few jingle bells jingling, too. And that's just outside. Inside cozy homes everywhere, the smells of freshly baked pies and cookies mingle with the scent of the freshly cut Christmas tree adorned with twinkling lights, sparkling ornaments, and candy canes. A ham or a bird roasting in the oven raises everyone's appetite for the big sit-down meal that draws generations of family, loved ones, and good friends to the table.

What better way to spend time with the family than cooking up delicious treats, making gifts for others, and fashioning your own unique Christmas decorations? As the weather turns chilly and the days get shorter, the weeks leading up to Christmas are the perfect time to start your craft projects—whether you're making gifts or home decorations.

Decorations, such as the Christmas Wreath, or a Decorative Jar make lovely gifts for those hard-to-buy-for people on your list. Homemade Christmas cards, such as the Christmas Snowflake Card, come in handy when it's time to put Christmas and New Year greetings in the mail. Gift Tags and Gift Decorations, too, are both useful and a fun way to add a personal touch to your gift presentations.

Set a festive scene in your home with Handmade Stockings, Christmas Card Tree Decorations, a Country-Style Garland, and a Decorative Centerpiece. And if you're feeling romantic, don't forget to hang a sprig or two of mistletoe.

The best cold-weather activity of all just might be staying indoors and cooking up delicious treats—either to give as gifts or serve to guests. From the Christmas Kitchen offers plenty of delectable gift ideas. From Indulgent Peppermint Hot Chocolate Mix and Pistachio & Apricot Nougat to Christmas Ginger Thins and Nutty Peppermint Bark, there's a sweet treat to appeal to everyone on your list. Not-so-sweet options, such as Corn Relish or Mixed Nuts in Herbed Salt, are sure to delight those who don't go for sugary treats.

Once your gifts are all wrapped up, it's time to plan for the festive meals. No matter what type of affair you envision, our festive recipes will do the season justice. The Christmas Favorites chapter includes essential recipes

for the main event—Festive Shrimp Cocktail, Traditional Roasted Turkey, Baked Fish, Creamed Spinach, Cornbread, and many other seasonal favorites.

Brunch favorites, including Christmas Spiced Pancakes, Asparagus & Egg Pastries, and the always-popular Pain au Chocolat Cinnamon Rolls, are sure to delight on Christmas morning.

Kick off a celebratory dinner with Chestnut & Pancetta Soup or Baked Oregano Lobster. For the main dish, choose from a traditional Prime Rib of Beef au Jus or Roasted Monkfish with Scalloped Potatoes. Pair these with superb sides, such as Mashed Sweet Potatoes. Desserts, including Cheesecake with Caramel Pecans or a Dark Chocolate Yule Log, provide an elegant ending.

We've even got you covered for drinks and canapés, with recipes for Holiday Eggnog, Kir Royale, Stuffed Olives, Blinis with Shrimp & Wasabi Cream, and more.

A chapter on leftovers offers deliciously creative ideas for giving them a second life. Turn leftover roasted turkey into Turkey Club Sandwiches, leftover roasted chicken into Chicken & Dumplings, leftover ham into Ham & Leek Risotto, and leftover potatoes and Brussels sprouts into Salmon & Potato Casserole.

Enjoy the Season

Christmas is meant to be full of joy and good fun, but too often we get hung up in all the preparation. So many parties to plan—and attend—so many meals to cook, gifts to buy or make, and other tasks to do. However, a good plan of action can mean that you'll enjoy the season to the utmost.

Start your crafting and shopping early—as soon as the mood strikes. The minute the weather turns chilly is the perfect time to start thinking about Christmas crafts. For gifts, the advice is to start early. However, if you have just a month to go and can brave the crowds, take advantage of the after-Thanksgiving sales. Better yet, if you're really organized, shop during the after-Christmas sales for next year's gifts. Even if you simply take

advantage of reductions on gift wrap, greeting and gift cards, Christmas tree ornaments, lights, and other decorations, you'll cut down on last-minute chores and save money.

As for the big day itself—or any parties you plan to throw for the season—the first order of business is to decide what type of holiday affair you want to host. Will it be a fancy black-tie soirée with champagne and caviar and guests in their holiday finery? Or do you prefer a cozier, family dinner with roasted turkey served with creamed spinach and finished off with pumpkin pie? Of course, there are a million options in between, including a casual cocktail party, a buffet party, a themed brunch, or a formal sit-down dinner.

Once you've settled on the event, start getting organized:

• **Create a guest list:** Decide how many people you'll invite. Will it be an intimate dinner for family and friends or would you prefer an open house with dozens of guests?

• **Send invitations:** Everyone is pulled in many different directions during this busy season, so send invitations well in advance—four to six weeks is ideal—and ask for RSVPs by a stated deadline.

• **Decide on a menu:** Once you know how many people are coming, put together a scrumptious menu that will suit your crowd.

• *Make ahead:* Casseroles, soups, cookies, and cakes can often be made ahead of time and stashed in the refrigerator for a day or two, or in the freezer for much longer. Soups, such as our Spiced Pumpkin Soup, freeze well. Mini quiches, tarts, most cookies and cakes, and cranberry sauce can be made well in advance and frozen until they're needed.

• *Order special food items:* Butchers sell out of their regular supply at this time of year, so be sure to order the meat you need—whether it's a giant turkey or a prime rib, or sausage meat for stuffing. If you plan to serve cake from a local bakery, it, too, should be ordered in advance.

• *Map out a time line for the preceding week:* Build a plan of action that starts at least a week in advance of your event. List tasks that can be tackled well ahead of time, such as purchasing any decoration (candles, place cards, etc.) or polishing the silver, and then move on to the items that must be accomplished closer to the event, such as shopping for ingredients. Plan which items you'll accomplish each day of the week leading up to the event.

• *Map out a day-of-event time line:* To make sure you're ready to go when that first guest rings the doorbell, map out a time line for the day of your event. Plan when to take foods out of the freezer to thaw, when to begin preheating your oven, and when to put the roast in.

• *Enjoy!* Once your party begins, relax and remember to enjoy the moment. If you've done the work ahead of time, your guests are sure to enjoy themselves and you should, too.

The most important—and truly the most magnificent—thing about the Christmas season is having a chance to celebrate the joy of the season with those you love. Embrace the crisp weather, the aromas and flavors, the colors and twinkling lights, and the utter joy of Christmas through crafts and recipes.

Christmas Favorites

* * * * * *

Spiced Pumpkin Soup

A deliciously warming and luxuriously creamy soup that's perfect to start off your Christmas dinner.

SERVES 4   PREP 20 MINS, PLUS COOLING   COOK 35–40 MINS

2 tablespoons olive oil

1 onion, chopped

1 garlic clove, chopped

1 tablespoon chopped fresh ginger

1 small red chile, seeded and finely chopped

2 tablespoons chopped fresh cilantro

1 bay leaf

8 cups seeded and diced pumpkin or butternut squash (about 2 pounds)

2½ cups vegetable broth

salt and pepper (optional)

light cream and chopped fresh cilantro, to garnish

1. Heat the oil in a large saucepan over medium heat. Add the onion and garlic and sauté for about 4 minutes, until slightly soft. Add the ginger, chile, cilantro, bay leaf, and pumpkin and cook for an additional 3 minutes.

2. Pour in the broth and bring to a boil. Skim any foam from the surface, if necessary. Reduce the heat and simmer, stirring occasionally, for about 25 minutes, or until the pumpkin is tender. Remove from the heat, remove and discard the bay leaf, and let the soup cool.

3. Transfer to a food processor or blender, in batches if necessary, and process until smooth. Return the mixture to the rinsed-out pan and season to taste with salt and pepper, if using.

4. Reheat gently, then remove from the heat and pour into warm soup bowls. Garnish each bowl with a swirl of cream and some chopped cilantro and serve immediately.

Tip DON'T DISCARD THE PUMPKIN SEEDS. PREHEAT THE OVEN TO 275°F, THEN RINSE AND DRY THE SEEDS, PUT THEM ONTO A LINED BAKING SHEET, AND TOSS WITH OIL AND SALT. COOK IN THE PREHEATED OVEN FOR 15 MINUTES, UNTIL GOLDEN BROWN. THEY WILL MAKE A DELICIOUS AND HEALTHY SNACK.

1

2

3

Festive Shrimp Cocktail

This classic appetizer has never lost its appeal. Creamy avocado and full-flavored shrimp are complemented by a hearty mayonnaise.

SERVES 8   PREP 25 MINS   COOK NONE

½ cup ketchup

1 teaspoon chili sauce

1 teaspoon
Worcestershire sauce

2 ruby grapefruits

8 lettuce leaves, shredded

2¼ pounds cooked
jumbo shrimp, peeled
and deveined

2 avocados, peeled,
pitted, and diced

lime slices and fresh
dill sprigs, to garnish

MAYONNAISE

2 extra-large egg yolks

1 teaspoon dry
English mustard

1 teaspoon salt

pinch of pepper

1¼ cups peanut oil

1 teaspoon white wine vinegar

1. To make the mayonnaise, put the egg yolks into a bowl, add the dry mustard, salt, and pepper, and beat together well. Begin whisking the egg yolks, adding the oil just one drop at a time, making sure that this has been thoroughly absorbed before adding another drop and whisking well.

2. Continue adding the oil, one drop at a time, until the mixture thickens and stiffens. At this point, whisk in the vinegar, then continue to dribble in the remaining oil slowly in a thin stream, whisking constantly, until you have used all the oil and you have a thick mayonnaise.

3. Mix together the mayonnaise, ketchup, chili sauce, and Worcestershire sauce in a small bowl. Cover with plastic wrap and refrigerate until required.

4. Cut off a slice from the top and bottom of each grapefruit, then peel off the skin and all the white pith. Cut between the membranes to separate the segments.

5. When ready to serve, make a bed of shredded lettuce in the bottom of eight glass dishes. Divide the shrimp, grapefruit segments, and avocados among them and spoon the mayonnaise dressing over the top. Serve the cocktails garnished with lime slices and dill sprigs.

1

3

4

Traditional Roasted Turkey

For many families, this magnificent bird is the centerpiece of the festive meal, often served with roasted potatoes, gravy, and Brussels sprouts.

SERVES 4   PREP 25 MINS   COOK 3 HRS 15 MINS, PLUS STANDING

11-pound oven-ready turkey
1 garlic clove, finely chopped
½ cup red wine
6 tablespoons butter, diced
seasonal vegetables, to serve

STUFFING

1½ cups chopped button mushrooms
1 onion, chopped
1 garlic clove, chopped
6 tablespoons butter
2 cups fresh bread crumbs
2 tablespoons finely chopped fresh sage
1 tablespoon lemon juice
salt and pepper (optional)

PORT & CRANBERRY SAUCE

½ cup sugar
1 cup port
2 cups fresh cranberries

1. Preheat the oven to 400°F.

2. To make the stuffing, put the mushrooms into a saucepan with the onion, garlic, and butter and cook for 3 minutes. Remove from the heat and stir in the remaining stuffing ingredients. Fill the neck end of the turkey with the stuffing and truss with string.

3. Put the turkey into a roasting pan. Rub the garlic over the bird, then pour the wine over it. Dot with the butter and roast in the preheated oven for 30 minutes. Baste, then reduce the temperature to 350°F and roast for an additional 40 minutes. Baste again and cover with aluminum foil. Roasted for an additional 2 hours, basting regularly. Check that the bird is cooked by inserting the tip of a sharp knife between the legs and body. If the juices run clear, it is cooked. Remove from the oven, loosely cover with foil, and let stand for 25 minutes.

4. Meanwhile, to make the sauce, put the sugar, port, and cranberries into a saucepan. Heat over medium heat until almost boiling. Serve the turkey with seasonal vegetables, if using, and the port and cranberry sauce.

Ham Steaks with Caramelized Apples

Applesauce is a natural with ham, and, when you make your own using freshly sautéed apple slices, it becomes a whole other experience.

SERVES 4	PREP 20 MINS	COOK 15 MINS

¼ cup firmly packed light brown sugar

1 tablespoon apple cider vinegar

1 cup hard apple cider or juice

small pinch of cinnamon

2 teaspoons Dijon mustard

3 tablespoons unsalted butter

4 firm cooking apples, such as Granny Smiths, peeled, cored, cut into quarters, and each quarter cut into 4 slices (16 slices per apple)

salt and pepper, to taste

2 pounds cooked ham steaks, cut into serving-size pieces, or freshly baked ham slices

1. In a small bowl, whisk together the brown sugar, apple cider vinegar, hard apple cider, cinnamon, and Dijon mustard. Reserve until needed.

2. Melt 2 tablespoons of the butter in a large skillet over high heat. About 30 seconds after the butter melts, add the apples. Sauté for 3–4 minutes, or until the edges are slightly browned.

3. Pour in the reserved apple cider mixture, turn the heat down to medium-high, and cook until the apples are tender and the liquid has reduced down to a glaze. If the liquid begins to get too thick before the apples are tender, add a splash of water and continue cooking.

4. Taste and season with salt and pepper to taste. Melt a tablespoon of butter in the skillet, and gently warm the ham steaks over medium-low heat. (The ham is already cooked, so you just want it warmed up, not recooked.) Serve with the hot apples spooned over the top.

Corned Beef & Cabbage

This one-dish wonder is an easy meal that is ideal for Christmas Day or anytime over the holiday season.

SERVES 6–10   PREP 20 MINS   COOK 3 HRS 15 MINS, PLUS RESTING

3½–5 pound corned beef brisket

1 spice packet sold with the corned beef brisket

1 bay leaf

1 teaspoon coarsely ground black pepper

salt, to taste

8 white round potatoes (about 2 pounds), cut in quarters

4 carrots, peeled and cut in chunks

1 onions, diced

3 celery stalks, diced

1 small green cabbage, cored and cut in 8 wedges

1. Put the corned beef, contents of the spice packet, bay leaf, pepper, and salt to taste into a large saucepan along with 12 cups of cold water. Cover and bring to a boil over high heat. Turn down the heat to low and slowly simmer for 2½ hours.

2. Add the potatoes, carrots, onions, and celery. Simmer, covered, for 20 minutes. Add the cabbage and cook covered for an additional 20 minutes, or until the potatoes and vegetables are tender. Remove the beef and let rest for 5 minutes. Slice against the grain and serve with the cabbage, potatoes, vegetables, and some of the cooking liquid. Serve with rye or dark bread and mustard on the side.

Roasted Turkey Breast

For an alternative to a whole turkey on Christmas Day, roasted turkey breast is a smaller and quicker way to still enjoy this traditional meat.

SERVES 4   PREP 30 MINS   COOK 1 HR 5 MINS, PLUS RESTING

1 bone-in turkey breast half

HERB RUB

2 tablespoons butter, softened

2 tablespoons olive oil

1 teaspoon lemon juice

1 garlic clove, minced

1 tablespoon chopped fresh parsley

1 teaspoon chopped fresh thyme leaves

1 teaspoon chopped fresh rosemary leaves

¼ teaspoon dried sage or poultry seasoning

cranberry sauce, to serve

salt and pepper, to taste

1. Preheat the oven to 425°F. Add the herb rub ingredients to a small bowl and whisk to combine. Use a boning knife to remove the breast from the breastbone and ribcage (or have the butcher do it). Place the breast, skin side down, on the cutting board. Fold the tenderloin toward the thinner side of the breast. Use the boning knife to make a slice into the thickest part of the breast, creating a shallow flap. Be careful not to cut all the way through.

2. Season generously with salt and pepper. Rub on the herb mixture. Fold the tenderloin back over into the center of the breast and gather together.

3. Take a piece of cooking twine and tie a simple knot around the breast at the thickest point. Repeat this every inch or so, until the breast is trussed into a nice, round, tight package. Flip over, skin side up, and place in a lightly oiled shallow roasting pan. Rub any leftover herb rub over the skin, and season with salt and fresh ground black pepper to taste.

4. Roast the turkey for 20 minutes, then reduce the heat to 325°F and continue roasting for about 45 minutes, until a thermometer registers 165°F when inserted into the thickest area of the breast. The juices should run clear and there should be no sign of pink when the tip of a sharp knife is inserted into the thickest part of the meat.

5. When the turkey's done, cover loosely with aluminum foil and let rest for 15 minutes before slicing and serving with any juices that collected in the pan. Serve with cranberry sauce.

21

Baked Fish

*This dish is perfect if you're feeding a large crowd—just scale up the
ingredients and use a second roasting dish.*

SERVES 4   PREP 30 MINS   COOK 40 MINS

*9–12 firm new potatoes
(about 1 pound),
thinly sliced*

1 large garlic clove, minced

2 onions, thinly sliced

*2 tablespoons olive oil, plus
extra for greasing*

*2 whole sea bass, red
snapper, or Alaskan pollock
(6–7 ounces each), heads
removed, scaled, gutted,
and well rinsed*

4 fresh thyme sprigs

½ lemon, sliced

*1½ cups sliced, pitted ripe
black olives*

salt and pepper, to taste

lemon wedges, to serve

1. Preheat the oven to 425°F and grease a roasting dish large enough to hold the fish and potatoes.

2. Arrange the potatoes, garlic, and onions in a layer on the bottom of the dish, drizzle with half of the oil, and season with salt and pepper. Tightly cover the dish with aluminum foil and bake in the preheated oven for 30 minutes, until the potatoes are almost tender.

3. Meanwhile, make three slashes on each side of the fish and rub salt and pepper into the slashes. Divide the thyme sprigs and lemon slices among the fish slashes, then set aside.

4. Reduce the oven temperature to 375°F. Uncover the dish and stir the olives into the potatoes. Arrange the fish on top, drizzle with the remaining oil, return to the oven, and cook for 10 minutes per 1 inch of fish thickness, or until the fish is cooked through and the flesh flakes easily.

5. Remove the dish from the oven. Fillet and skin the fish and divide the fillets among four warm plates. Serve with the potatoes, onions, and olives, along with lemon wedges for squeezing over the fish.

23

Macaroni & Cheese

A traditional favorite at the holiday dinner table, this dish is a real crowd pleaser and makes a great accompaniment to Christmas dinner.

SERVES 4–6   *PREP 20 MINS*   *COOK 40 MINS*

6 ounces macaroni

4 tablespoons butter, plus extra for greasing

1½ tablespoons all-purpose flour

½ teaspoon dry mustard

1¾ cups milk, warmed

2 cups shredded cheddar or Swiss cheese

1½ cups diced, skinless cooked turkey

1 red bell pepper, preserved in olive oil, drained, and thinly sliced

2 tablespoons chopped parsley

pinch of cayenne pepper (optional)

⅓ cup fine dry bread crumbs

salt and pepper

1. Preheat the oven to 400°F. Grease a baking pan, then set aside. Bring a large saucepan of salted water to a boil. Add the macaroni and cook for 2 minutes less than specified in the package directions. Drain well, rinse under cold water, and shake vigorously to remove the water.

2. Meanwhile, melt 2 tablespoons of the butter in a large saucepan over medium heat. Sprinkle in the flour and dry mustard and stir for 2 minutes. Remove the pan from the heat and slowly stir in the milk, stirring continuously so no lumps form.

3. Return the saucepan to the heat and simmer, stirring, for 3 minutes, or until the sauce is smooth and thick. Add 1½ cups of the cheese and stir until it melts. Add the macaroni, turkey, bell pepper, parsley, and cayenne pepper, if using, and season to taste. Gently stir all the ingredients together.

4. Spoon the mixture into the prepared baking pan. Mix the bread crumbs with the reserved cheese, then sprinkle with the surface. Dot the top with the remaining butter and place the pan on a baking sheet.

5. Bake in the preheated oven for 25 minutes, or until piping hot and the top is golden brown.

Creamed Spinach

This simple but deliciously creamy spinach is a classic accompaniment to steak, but it is also good with roasted meats.

1 stick unsalted butter

2 (12-ounce) packages prewashed, ready-to-use baby spinach

½ onion, finely diced

⅓ cup all-purpose flour

3 cloves garlic, finely minced

1½ cups cold milk

pinch freshly ground nutmeg

salt and pepper, to taste

1. Put a large saucepan over high heat. Add 1 tablespoon of the butter, and as soon as it melts, add all the spinach and cover quickly. Let cook for 1 minute, uncover, and continue cooking, stirring the spinach with a long wooden spoon, until just barely wilted. Transfer to a colander to drain.

2. When the spinach is cool enough to handle, squeeze out as much liquid as possible, and coarsely chop. Press between paper towels to draw out the last of the water, and reserve until needed.

3. Melt the rest of the butter in a saucepan over medium heat. Add the onions and sauté for about 5 minutes, or until translucent. Whisk in the flour and cook for 3 minutes, stirring. Add the garlic and cook for 1 minute. Pour in the cold milk, whisking constantly, and cook until it comes to a simmer. Reduce heat to low and simmer for another 5 minutes. The sauce will thicken as it cooks.

4. Season the sauce with nutmeg, salt, and black pepper to taste. Add the spinach and stir to combine. The dish is ready to serve as soon as the spinach is heated through. Taste and adjust seasoning before serving.

Cinnamon Swirl
Sour Cream Bundt Cake

This cake is ideal for the holiday season, because you'll always have a delicious slice of cake ready to offer any unexpected guests that stop by.

SERVES 6–8   PREP 30 MINS   COOK 50 MINS, PLUS COOKING

2½ cups all-purpose flour, plus extra for dusting

1 teaspoon baking powder

1 teaspoon baking soda

½ teaspoon salt

1½ sticks unsalted butter, plus extra for greasing

1½ cups granulated sugar

3 extra-large eggs

1 cup sour cream

1 teaspoon vanilla extract

½ cup chopped walnuts, optional

FOR THE SWIRL

1 tablespoon ground cinnamon

3 tablespoons packed light brown sugar

2 tablespoons granulated sugar

FOR THE GLAZE

1 cup confectioners' sugar

about 1½ tablespoons milk

1 teaspoon ground cinnamon, or to taste

1. Preheat oven to 350°F. Grease a 10-inch Bundt pan and lightly dust with flour. Mix together the flour, baking powder, baking soda, and salt in a mixing bowl.

2. Cream the butter and sugar together in a separate large mixing bowl until light and fluffy. Beat in the eggs, one at a time, mixing thoroughly before adding the next. Beat in the sour cream and vanilla until combined. Add the flour mixture, stirring just until combined. Stir in the walnuts, if using.

3. Pour half the batter into the prepared pan and spread evenly. Mix the ingredients for the swirl in a small bowl, then sprinkle the mixture evenly around the center of the batter. Cover with the rest of the batter.

4. Bake in the preheated oven for 50 minutes, or until a toothpick inserted into the center comes out clean. Let cool 20 minutes before removing from the pan.

5. For the glaze, add the confectioners' sugar to a small mixing bowl and stir in enough milk to create a thick, but pourable glaze. Stir in the cinnamon to taste. Drizzle the glaze over the top of the cake. Once it has set, slice and serve.

Cornbread

This cornbread is one of the traditional stars of Christmas. A warm, freshly cut wedge of this during the holiday season is a magical thing.

SERVES 9	PREP 30 MINS	COOK 30–35 MINS, PLUS COOLING

vegetable oil, for brushing
1½ cups all-purpose flour
1 teaspoon salt
4 teaspoons baking powder
1 teaspoon superfine sugar
2½ cups yellow cornmeal
1½ sticks butter, softened
4 eggs
1 cup milk
3 tablespoons heavy cream

1. Preheat the oven to 400°F. Brush an 8-inch square cake pan with oil.

2. Sift together the flour, salt, and baking powder into a bowl. Add the sugar and cornmeal and stir to mix. Add the butter and cut it into the dry ingredients with a knife, then rub in with your fingertips until the mixture resembles bread crumbs.

3. Lightly beat the eggs with the milk and cream in a small bowl, then stir into the cornmeal mixture until thoroughly combined.

4. Spoon the batter into the prepared pan and smooth the surface. Bake for 30–35 minutes, until a toothpick inserted into the center of the bread comes out clean. Remove the pan from the oven and let the bread cool for 5–10 minutes, then cut into squares and serve warm.

Ambrosia

A delicious fruit salad fit for Christmas, made with oranges, pineapple, coconut, and jewel-like maraschino cherries.

SERVES 6	PREP 15 MINS	COOK NONE

8 navel oranges

1 (8-ounce) can pineapple pieces, drained

2 tablespoons confectioners' sugar

¾ cup flaked coconut

⅓ cup halved maraschino cherries

1. Peel the oranges and separate the sections over a small bowl to catch the juice, then cut the orange sections in half and set juice aside.

2. Combine the oranges and pineapple in a large bowl. Sprinkle with the sugar, coconut, and cherries and toss together gently until combined. Pour ¼ cup of the reserved orange juice over the fruit mixture. Cover and refrigerate until ready to serve.

Pumpkin Pie

This delicious sweet pie is a firm Christmas favorite. This version uses a crunchy streusel topping made with cinnamon and nuts.

SERVES 6   PREP 45 MINS, PLUS CHILLING   COOK 2 HRS 20 MINS

1 small sweet pumpkin or 2 butternut squash (about 4 pounds)

1 cup all-purpose flour, plus extra for dusting

¼ teaspoon baking powder

1½ teaspoons ground cinnamon

¾ teaspoon ground nutmeg

¾ teaspoon ground cloves

1 teaspoon salt

½ cup superfine sugar

4 tablespoons cold unsalted butter, diced, plus extra for greasing

3 eggs

1¾ cups canned sweetened condensed milk

½ teaspoon vanilla extract

1 tablespoon raw brown sugar

STREUSEL TOPPING

2 tablespoons all-purpose flour

¼ cup raw brown sugar

1 teaspoon ground cinnamon

2 tablespoons cold unsalted butter, cut into small pieces

⅔ cup chopped pecans

⅔ cup chopped walnuts

1. Preheat the oven to 375°F. Halve the pumpkin, then remove and discard the stem, seeds, and stringy insides. Put the pumpkin halves, face down, in a shallow roasting pan and cover with aluminum foil. Bake in the preheated oven for 1½ hours, then let cool. Scoop out the flesh and puree in a food processor. Drain off any excess liquid. Cover with plastic wrap, and chill until ready to use.

2. Grease a 9-inch round pie plate. Sift the flour and baking powder into a large bowl. Stir in ½ teaspoon of the cinnamon, ¼ teaspoon of the nutmeg, ¼ teaspoon of the cloves, ½ teaspoon of the salt, and all of the superfine sugar until combined.

3. Rub in the butter with your fingertips until the mixture resembles fine bread crumbs, then make a well in the center. Lightly beat one of the eggs and pour it into the well. Mix together with a wooden spoon, then use your hands to shape the dough into a ball. Place the dough on a lightly floured work surface and roll out to a circle large enough to line the pie plate. Use it to line the plate, then trim the edges. Cover with plastic wrap and chill in the refrigerator for 30 minutes.

4. Preheat the oven to 425°F. To make the filling, put the pumpkin puree into a large bowl, then stir in the condensed milk and the remaining eggs. Add the remaining spices and salt, then stir in the vanilla extract and brown sugar. Pour into the pastry shell and bake in the preheated oven for 15 minutes.

5. Meanwhile, make the streusel topping. Combine the flour, sugar, and cinnamon in a bowl, rub in the butter, then stir in the nuts. Remove the pie from the oven and reduce the heat to 350°F. Sprinkle with the topping, then bake for an additional 35 minutes.

Crème Brûlée

This is crème brûlée with a twist—delicious soft fruit lies waiting to be discovered under the crisp caramelized topping and creamy layer beneath.

SERVES 6   PREP 15 MINS   COOK 5 MINS, PLUS CHILLING

1½–2 cups mixed soft fruits, such as blueberries and pitted fresh cherries (about 8 ounces)

1½–2 tablespoons orange liqueur

1 cup mascarpone cheese

1 cup crème fraîche

2–3 tablespoons packed dark brown sugar

1. Put the fruit into the bottom of six ⅔-cup ramekins (individual ceramic dishes), then sprinkle the liqueur over the fruit.

2. Cream the mascarpone cheese in a bowl until soft, then gradually beat in the crème fraîche.

3. Spoon the cheese mixture over the fruit, smoothing the surface and making sure that the tops are level. Chill in the refrigerator for at least 2 hours.

4. Sprinkle the tops with the sugar. Using a chef's blowtorch, heat the tops for 2–3 minutes, until caramelized. Alternatively, cook under a preheated broiler, turning the dishes, for 3–4 minutes, or until the tops are lightly caramelized all over.

5. Serve warm or chill in the refrigerator for 15–20 minutes before serving.

Tip YOU COULD VARY THE FRUIT ACCORDING TO TASTE. SOFT FRUIT IS BEST, SO USE CHOPPED PITTED FRESH APRICOTS, PEACHES, OR PLUMS, OR A COMBINATION OF ANY OF THESE. MIXED BERRIES ARE ALSO A PERFECT COMPLEMENT TO THIS LUSCIOUS AND CREAMY DESSERT.

Christmas Morning

* * * * * *

Rich Orange Crepes

If you like pancakes for breakfast, you'll love these light and luscious buttery crepes, richly flavored with juicy oranges on Christmas Day.

SERVES 4   PREP 15 MINS   COOK 10 MINS

1¼ cups all-purpose flour

1 cup milk

1 extra-large egg

3 tablespoons orange juice

2 tablespoons butter, melted

½ tablespoon butter, melted, for frying

2 oranges, peeled and divided into sections, to serve

ORANGE BUTTER

4 tablespoons unsalted butter

finely grated zest and juice of 1 orange

1 tablespoon sugar

1. To make the crepes, put the flour, milk, egg, orange juice, and butter into a mixing bowl and beat until smooth. Alternatively, process in a food processor until smooth.

2. Heat a crepe pan or heavy skillet until hot, lightly brush with melted butter, and pour in a small ladleful of batter, swirling to thinly coat the surface of the pan.

3. Cook the crepe until golden underneath, then turn and cook the other side. Repeat this process, using the remaining batter and brushing the pan with butter as necessary; keep the cooked crepes warm in a low oven.

4. To make the orange butter, melt the butter in a small saucepan, add the orange zest, orange juice, and sugar, and stir until the sugar has dissolved. Simmer, stirring, for 30 seconds, then remove from the heat.

5. Serve the crepes folded over, with the orange sections and the orange butter poured over the top.

Apple & Spice Oatmeal

What better way to set yourself up for Christmas Day than with this delicious and wholesome oatmeal, full of warm, spicy goodness.

SERVES 4 .... PREP 5 MINS .... COOK 15 MINS

2½ cups milk

1 teaspoon salt

1¼ cups rolled oats

2 crisp, sweet apples, such as Pippin or Golden Delicious

½ teaspoon ground allspice

honey, to serve

1. Put the milk into a saucepan and bring to a boil. Add the salt and sprinkle in the oats, stirring constantly.

2. Reduce the heat to low and let the oats simmer for 10 minutes, stirring occasionally.

3. Meanwhile, peel, halve, core, and grate the apples. When the oatmeal is creamy and most of the liquid has evaporated, stir in the grated apple and allspice. Spoon into serving bowls and drizzle with honey.

Tip IF YOU DON'T LIKE THE RICH CREAMINESS OF OATMEAL MADE WITH MILK, YOU CAN ALWAYS SUBSTITUTE IT WITH AN EQUAL QUANTITY OF WATER, AND JUST SERVE THE OATMEAL WITH MILK OR CREAM FOR POURING. YOU COULD ALSO TRY SERVING IT WITH MAPLE SYRUP FOR A REALLY SWEET HIT.

1

2

3

Christmas Spiced Pancakes

With Christmas flavors of cranberries and nuts and the indulgence of a rum-infused syrup, these pancakes are definitely worth making.

SERVES 4 — PREP 10 MINS, PLUS STANDING — COOK 20 MINS

1¼ cups all-purpose flour
1½ teaspoons baking powder
pinch of salt
1 teaspoon allspice
1 cup milk
1 extra-large egg
2 tablespoons melted butter
1 cup chopped cranberries
¼ cup chopped candied peel
¼ cup hazelnuts, chopped
1 tablespoon sunflower oil, for oiling
2 tablespoons packed dark brown sugar
¼ cup water
3 tablespoons dark rum
1 teaspoon vanilla extract

1. Sift the flour, baking powder, salt, and allspice into a bowl. Add the milk, egg, and butter and beat until smooth. Stir in the cranberries, candied peel, and hazelnuts and let stand for 5 minutes.

2. Lightly oil a flat griddle pan or skillet and heat over a medium heat. Spoon tablespoons of the batter onto the pan to make oval shapes, and cook until bubbles appear on the surface.

3. Turn over with a spatula and cook the other side until golden brown. Repeat this process, using the remaining batter, while keeping the cooked pancakes warm in a low oven.

4. Put the sugar and water into a small saucepan and heat over low heat, stirring, until the sugar has dissolved. Bring to a boil and boil for 1 minute, then add the rum and vanilla extract and bring back to a boil. Remove from the heat.

5. Spoon the syrup over the pancakes and serve immediately.

Mushrooms & Sage on Sourdough Toast

Sourdough bread is substantial and filling, making this hearty breakfast a good choice if you have a long day of festivities ahead.

....
SERVES 4   PREP 10 MINS   COOK 10 MINS
....

⅓ cup olive oil

2 tablespoons coarsely chopped fresh sage, plus 16–20 whole small leaves

1 pound cremini mushrooms of equal size, halved

squeeze of lemon juice

1 large garlic clove, thinly sliced

2 tablespoons chopped fresh flat-leaf parsley

¼ teaspoon pepper

pinch of sea salt flakes

4 slices sourdough bread

Parmesan cheese shavings, to garnish

1. Heat the oil in a large skillet over medium–high heat. Add the chopped sage and sizzle for a few seconds. Add the mushrooms and sauté for 3–4 minutes, or until they are beginning to release their juices.

2. Add the lemon juice, then add the garlic, parsley, pepper, and salt. Cook for an additional 5 minutes.

3. Meanwhile, toast the bread on both sides. Place on warm plates and pile the mushrooms on top.

4. Sizzle the whole sage leaves in the oil remaining in the pan over high heat for a few seconds, until crisp. Sprinkle them over the mushrooms and garnish with cheese shavings.

Poached Eggs with Spinach & Cheddar

Guests coming for Christmas Day brunch? Serve this easy spin on eggs Florentine as a delicious yet simple festive treat.

SERVES 4   PREP 10 MINS   COOK 15 MINS

1 tablespoon olive oil

1 (6-ounce) package fresh
baby spinach leaves

4 thick slices ciabatta bread

2 tablespoons butter

4 extra-large eggs

1 cup shredded cheddar cheese

salt and pepper (optional)

freshly grated nutmeg, to serve

1. Preheat the broiler to high. Heat the oil in a wok or large saucepan, add the spinach, and stir-fry for 2–3 minutes, until the leaves are wilted. Drain in a colander, season to taste with salt and pepper, if using, and keep warm.

2. Toast the bread on both sides until golden. Spread one side of each slice with butter and place, buttered side up, in a baking dish.

3. Meanwhile, fill a deep skillet with boiling water and bring back to a boil. Reduce the heat to a gentle simmer. Break the eggs into the water and poach for 2–3 minutes, until the whites are set. Remove from the pan with a draining spoon.

4. Arrange the spinach on the toast and top each slice with a poached egg. Sprinkle with the grated cheese. Cook under the preheated broiler for 1–2 minutes, until the cheese has melted. Sprinkle with nutmeg and serve immediately.

1

2

4

43

Smoked Salmon & Egg on Toasted Muffin

Topped with an easy no-fail hollandaise sauce, this is the ultimate festive brunch dish for two.

SERVES 2   PREP 20 MINS   COOK 7–8 MINS

4 eggs

2 English muffins

½ tablespoon butter, for spreading

½ cup arugula

4 ounces smoked salmon, sliced

HOLLANDAISE SAUCE

2 extra-large egg yolks

2 teaspoons lemon juice

1 tablespoon white wine vinegar

1 stick unsalted butter

salt and pepper (optional)

1. To make the hollandaise sauce, put the egg yolks into a blender. Season with salt and pepper, if using, then process for a few seconds until thoroughly blended.

2. Put the lemon juice and vinegar into a small saucepan and heat until simmering. With the blender running, add the hot liquid in a slow, steady stream. Turn off the blender.

3. Put the butter into the pan and heat until melted and foaming. With the blender running, add the butter, a few drops at a time, until you have a smooth, thick sauce. Use a spatula to scrape down any sauce from the side of the blender, then process for an additional few seconds.

4. Fill a deep skillet with boiling water and bring back to a boil. Reduce the heat to a gentle simmer. Break the eggs into the water and poach for 2–3 minutes, until the whites are set. Remove from the pan with a slotted spoon. Halve and lightly toast the muffins.

5. Spread the toasted muffins with the butter and place on two serving plates. Top with nearly all the arugula and the slices of smoked salmon. Remove the eggs from the water with a slotted spoon, drain on paper towels, and place on top of the salmon. Spoon the warm sauce over the poached eggs. Garnish with pepper, if using, and the remaining arugula. Serve immediately.

Asparagus & Egg Pastries

Asparagus and eggs make a great pairing in any recipe. These quick-and-easy pastries are great for a Christmas brunch buffet.

SERVES 4   **PREP 30 MINS, PLUS CHILLING**   **COOK 20 MINS**

1 (1-pound) package ready-to-bake puff pastry, thawed if frozen

1 tablespoon flour, for dusting

1 tablespoon milk, for brushing

24 slim asparagus spears (about 10 ounces)

¾ cup store-bought tomato sauce

1 teaspoon hot smoked paprika

4 eggs

1. Roll out the pastry on a lightly floured surface to a 14 x 8-inch rectangle, then cut the pastry into four 8 x 3½-inch rectangles.

2. Line a baking sheet with nonstick parchment paper and place the pastry rectangles on the sheet. Prick all over with a fork and brush lightly with milk. Chill in the refrigerator for 20 minutes.

3. Snap off the woody ends of the asparagus and discard. Bring a saucepan of water to a boil. Add the asparagus, bring back to a boil, and cook for 2–3 minutes, until almost tender. Drain and refresh in cold water, then drain again and set aside.

4. Meanwhile, preheat the oven to 400°F. Mix the tomato sauce and paprika together and divide among the pastry crusts, spreading it out almost to the edges. Bake in the preheated oven for 10–12 minutes, until the pastry is puffed around the edges and pale golden.

5. Remove from the oven and arrange the asparagus on top, leaving space for an egg in the middle of each pastry.

6. Crack an egg into a cup and slide it into the space created. Repeat with the remaining eggs, then return the pastries to the oven for 8 minutes, or until the eggs are just set.

Potato Griddle Cakes

Serve these griddle cakes on their own, or as a side to your Christmas Day brunch. They are delicious with sour cream spooned over the top.

SERVES 8   PREP 10 MINS   COOK 15–20 MINS

9 russet or Yukon gold potatoes (about 2¼ pounds)

1 onion

3 tablespoons all-purpose flour

1 egg, beaten

2 tablespoons sunflower oil, for frying

salt and pepper (optional)

sour cream, to serve

1. Finely grate the potatoes and onion. Put them into a strainer and press out as much liquid as possible, then spread out on a clean dish towel. Roll up and twist the dish towel to remove any remaining moisture.

2. Put the grated vegetables into a bowl and stir in the flour. Stir in the egg and season with salt and pepper, if using.

3. Heat the oil in a flat griddle or skillet until medium-hot. Drop large spoons of the batter into the pan, pressing with a spatula to flatten, and cook in batches, turning once, for 8–10 minutes, until the griddle cakes are golden brown and cooked through.

4. Drain the griddle cakes on paper towels and keep warm while you cook the remaining mixture. Serve hot with some sour cream.

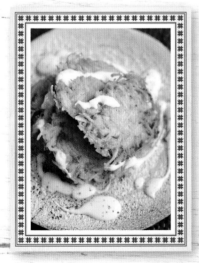

Eggs Baked in Tomatoes

Eggs and tomatoes are a wonderful combination—full-flavored beefsteak tomatoes make great nests for the eggs and their zesty cheese topping.

SERVES 4 · *PREP 10 MINS* · *COOK 20 MINS*

4 large beefsteak tomatoes

4 eggs

2 tablespoons chopped fresh oregano

¼ cup freshly grated Parmesan cheese

1 garlic clove, halved

4 slices country-style bread

2 tablespoons olive oil

salt and pepper (optional)

1. Preheat the oven to 425°F. Cut a slice from the top of each tomato and scoop out the seeds and pulp. Place the tomatoes, cut side up, in a baking dish or pan.

2. Break an egg into each tomato, then sprinkle with oregano, as well as salt and pepper, if using. Sprinkle with the cheese and bake in the preheated oven for about 20 minutes, or until the eggs are just set, with runny yolks.

3. Meanwhile, rub the garlic over the bread, put onto a baking sheet and drizzle with oil. Bake in the oven for 5–6 minutes, or until golden.

4. Put each tomato on a slice of bread and serve immediately.

✳ *Tip* ✳

KEEP AN EYE ON THE EGGS TO MAKE SURE THAT THEY DON'T OVERCOOK— THESE ARE DELICIOUS WHILE THE YOLKS ARE STILL A LITTLE RUNNY.

1

2

3

49

Pain au Chocolat Cinnamon Rolls

This is the ultimate French patisserie-style breakfast pastry.
Use a really good-quality dark chocolate for the best results.

SERVES 12   **PREP 10 MINS, PLUS CHILLING AND COOLING**   **COOK 30–35 MINS**

4 ounces semisweet chocolate,
broken into pieces

1 sheet ready-to-bake
puff pastry, thawed if frozen

2 tablespoons butter, melted

2 tablespoons sugar

1½ teaspoons
ground cinnamon

1. Put the chocolate into a heatproof bowl set over a saucepan of gently simmering water and heat until melted. Remove from the heat, stir until smooth, then let cool for 15 minutes, stirring occasionally.

2. Unroll the pastry and place on a board. Generously brush with some of the melted butter. Let stand for 10 minutes, then spread the cooled chocolate all over the buttered pastry. Mix the sugar and cinnamon together and sprinkle it over the chocolate.

3. Roll up the pastry from one long side, then brush all over with more of the melted butter. Chill in the refrigerator for 15 minutes. Preheat the oven to 425°F. Use the remaining butter to grease a 12-cup muffin pan.

4. Using a serrated knife, slice the pastry roll into 12 even circles. Place the circles, cut side up, in the prepared pan.

5. Bake in the preheated oven for 15–20 minutes, or until risen and golden brown. Let cool in the pan for 5 minutes, then transfer to a wire rack. Serve warm or cold.

Festive Appetizers

✳ ✳ ✳ ✳ ✳ ✳

Chestnut & Pancetta Soup

Chestnuts have a real taste of winter and the delicious mix of smoky pancetta, vegetables, creamy chestnuts, and rosemary makes a filling soup.

SERVES 6   PREP 15 MINS   COOK 45–50 MINS

3 tablespoons olive oil

6 ounces pancetta, cut into strips

2 onions, finely chopped

2 carrots, finely chopped

2 celery stalks, finely chopped

30 dried chestnuts (about 12 ounces), soaked overnight

2 garlic cloves, finely chopped

1 tablespoon finely chopped fresh rosemary

4 cups chicken broth

salt and pepper (optional)

1 tablespoon extra virgin olive oil, for drizzling

1. Heat the olive oil in a large saucepan, add the pancetta, and cook over medium heat, stirring frequently, for 2–3 minutes, until starting to brown.

2. Add the onions, carrots, and celery and cook, stirring frequently, for 10 minutes, or until light golden and soft.

3. Drain the chestnuts, add to the pan with the garlic and rosemary, and stir well. Pour in the broth, bring to a simmer, and cook, uncovered, for 30–35 minutes, until the chestnuts are beginning to soften and break down.

4. Season to taste with salt and pepper, if using. Ladle the soup into warm bowls, drizzle with extra virgin olive oil, and serve immediately.

Tip

THIS IS A GREAT STANDBY RECIPE FOR CHRISTMAS ENTERTAINING. IT CAN BE PREPARED UP TO TWO DAYS BEFORE YOU NEED TO SERVE IT—TRANSFER TO A BOWL, COVER WITH PLASTIC WRAP, AND CHILL IN THE REFRIGERATOR UNTIL NEEDED.

1

2

3

Gravadlax

This is a wonderful alternative to prepared smoked salmon. It takes a little time to prepare, but the result is worth it for a festive occasion.

SERVES 8–12   PREP 10 MINS, PLUS CHILLING   COOK NONE

2 salmon fillets (about 1 pound each), skin on

⅓ cup coarsely chopped fresh dill

½ cup sea salt

¼ cup sugar

1 tablespoon coarsely crushed white peppercorns

buttered whole-wheat bread, to serve

lemon wedges and fresh dill sprigs, to garnish

1. Rinse the salmon fillets under cold running water and dry with paper towels. Put one fillet, skin side down, into a nonmetallic dish.

2. Mix the dill, sea salt, sugar, and peppercorns together in a small bowl. Spread this mixture over the fillet in the dish and put the second fillet, skin side up, on top. Put a plate, the same size as the fish, on top and weigh down with three or four food cans.

3. Chill in the refrigerator for 2 days, turning the fish about every 12 hours and basting with any juices that come out of the fish.

4. Remove the salmon from the solution and thinly slice, without slicing the skin, as you would smoked salmon. Cut the buttered bread into triangles. Garnish the salmon with lemon wedges and dill sprigs, and serve.

1

2

4

Classic Melon, Prosciutto & Pecorino Salad

This classic salad makes a light and refreshing appetizer that won't fill you up too much before the Christmas main dish arrives.

SERVES 4   PREP 10 MINS   COOK NONE

⅛ small watermelon, peeled, seeded, and thinly sliced

½ honeydew melon, peeled, seeded, and thinly sliced

1 small canteloupe, peeled, seeded, and thinly sliced

5 ounces prosciutto, sliced

¼ cup pecorino cheese shavings

1 cup fresh basil

DRESSING

¼ cup light olive oil

¼ cup aged sherry vinegar

salt and pepper (optional)

1. Arrange the watermelon, honeydew melon, and canteloupe slices on a large serving platter.

2. Tear any large prosciutto slices in half, then fold them all over and around the melon.

3. To make the dressing, put the oil and vinegar into a screw-top jar, season well with salt and pepper, if using, screw on the lid, and shake well. Drizzle the dressing over the melon and ham.

4. Sprinkle with the cheese and basil and serve immediately.

Blue Cheese & Herb Pâté

Vegetarian guests will be delighted with this meat-free version of a classic Christmas Day appetizer. Serve with plenty of toast.

SERVES 4	PREP 15 MINS. PLUS CHILLING	COOK 5 MINS

⅔ cup vegetarian low-fat cream cheese

⅔ cup cottage cheese

⅔ cup plain yogurt

⅔ cup crumbled vegetarian blue cheese

⅓ cup dried cranberries, finely chopped

1 tablespoon each chopped fresh parsley, snipped fresh chives, chopped fresh dill, and chopped fresh tarragon

6 tablespoons butter

2 tablespoons chopped walnuts

toast, to serve

1. Beat the cream cheese to loosen, then gradually beat in the cottage cheese and yogurt until smooth. Add the blue cheese, cranberries, and herbs and stir together. Spoon the mixture into four ⅔-cup ramekins (individual ceramic dishes) and carefully smooth the tops.

2. Clarify the butter by gently heating it in a small saucepan until melted. Skim any foam off the surface and discard.

3. Carefully pour the clear yellow top layer into a small bowl, discarding the milky liquid left in the pan.

4. Pour a little of the clarified butter over the top of each ramekin and sprinkle with the walnuts. Chill for at least 30 minutes, until firm, then serve with toast.

Chicken Liver Pâté

This is a really rich pâté, so serve it sparingly if it's the starter for the big Christmas meal. Its creaminess is complemented by the crisp Melba toast.

SERVES 4–6   PREP 20 MINS, PLUS CHILLING   COOK 10 MINS

1¾ sticks butter

8 ounces trimmed chicken livers, thawed if frozen

2 tablespoons red wine

1½ teaspoons chopped fresh sage

1 garlic clove, coarsely chopped

⅔ cup heavy cream

salt and pepper (optional)

fresh sage leaves, to garnish

melba toast, to serve

1. Melt 3 tablespoons of the butter in a large, heavy skillet. Add the chicken livers and cook over medium heat for 4 minutes on each side. They should be brown on the outside but still pink in the center. Transfer to a food processor and process until finely chopped.

2. Add the red wine to the pan and stir, scraping up any sediment with a wooden spoon, then add to the food processor with the chopped sage, garlic, and 1 stick of the remaining butter. Process until smooth. Add the cream, season to taste with salt and pepper, if using, and process until thoroughly combined and smooth. Spoon the pâté into a dish or ramekins (individual ceramic dishes), smooth the surface, and let cool completely.

3. Melt the remaining butter in a small saucepan, then spoon it over the surface of the pâté, leaving any sediment in the pan. Let cool, then cover and chill in the refrigerator. Garnish with sage and serve with melba toast.

1

2

3

Mixed Antipasto Meat Platter

This useful make-ahead appetizer can be refrigerated for a couple of hours—but don't drizzle with the oil until you're just ready to serve.

1 cantaloupe

2 ounces Italian salami, thinly sliced

8 prosciutto slices

8 bresaola slices

8 mortadella slices

4 plum tomatoes, thinly sliced

4 fresh figs, halved

1 cup pitted ripe black olives

2 tablespoons shredded fresh basil leaves

¼ cup extra virgin olive oil

pepper (optional)

1 tablespoon extra virgin olive oil, for drizzling

1. Cut the melon in half, scoop out and discard the seeds, then cut the flesh into eight wedges. Arrange the wedges on one half of a large serving platter.

2. Arrange the salami, prosciutto, bresaola, and mortadella in loose folds on the other half of the platter. Arrange the tomato slices and fig halves on the platter.

3. Sprinkle the olives over the antipasto. Sprinkle the basil over the tomatoes and drizzle with olive oil. Season to taste with pepper, then drizzle with extra virgin olive oil and serve immediately.

❄ Variation ❄

IF YOU CAN'T FIND FRESH FIGS, YOU COULD USE ARTICHOKE HEARTS IN OLIVE OIL INSTEAD. MAKE SURE YOU BUY A GOOD-QUALITY BRAND, OTHERWISE YOU MAY END UP WITH WOODY PIECES.

62

Baked Oregano Lobster

This is the perfect appetizer when you really want to spare no expense. Once you've prepared the lobster, it's simple to put together.

❧

SERVES 4   PREP 30 MINS   COOK 30 MINS

4 frozen lobster tails
(about 6 ounces each),
thawed and patted dry

¼ cup olive oil

1 large shallot, minced

2 garlic cloves, minced

⅓ cup fine dry bread crumbs

2 teaspoons dried oregano

finely grated zest of 2 lemons

1 tablespoon finely chopped
fresh flat-leaf parsley

salt and pepper (optional)

1 tablespoon olive oil,
for drizzling

1. Preheat the oven to 350°F. Put a lobster tail on a board, shell down. Use scissors to cut lengthwise through the shell without cutting through the tail fan. Do not crush the shell. Use a small knife to cut the tail meat in half lengthwise without cutting through the shell. Cut away the cartilage on top of the shell. Use the tip of a knife to cut out the black intestinal vein. Repeat with the remaining tails. Cover and chill until required.

2. Heat the oil in a small skillet. Add the shallot and sauté for 1–2 minutes, until golden. Add the garlic and stir for an additional 1 minute, or until the shallot is soft. Stir in the bread crumbs, oregano, lemon zest, and parsley and season with salt and pepper, if using.

3. Lightly season inside the split tails with salt and pepper, if using, then place the tails in a deep roasting pan, using balls of aluminum foil to wedge them upright, if necessary. Divide the oregano mixture among them, lightly pressing it into the splits and covering half the tails. Drizzle with oil.

4. Add enough boiling water to the pan to come halfway up the sides of the tails. Bake in the preheated oven for 20 minutes, until the flesh at the thickest part of the tails is white. Remove from the oven and serve immediately.

Garlic-Stuffed Mushrooms

Pine nuts give these stuffed mushrooms a really crunchy texture, and dried apricots and feta cheese provide a tasty flavor combination.

SERVES 4	PREP 15 MINS	COOK 10–12 MINS

4 large portobello mushrooms

4 sprays olive oil

2–3 garlic cloves, crushed

2 shallots

½ cup fresh whole-wheat bread crumbs

8 fresh basil sprigs

3 tablespoons chopped dried apricots

1 tablespoon pine nuts

⅓ cup feta cheese

pepper (optional)

fresh basil sprigs, to garnish

1. Preheat the oven to 350°F. Remove the stems from the mushrooms and set aside. Spray the bottom of the mushrooms with the oil and place them, cap side down, in a roasting pan.

2. Put the mushroom stems into a food processor with the garlic, shallots, and bread crumbs. Put the basil sprigs in the food processor with the apricots, pine nuts, and cheese. Add pepper to taste, if using.

3. Process for 1–2 minutes, until the mixture has a stuffing consistency, then divide among the mushroom caps.

4. Bake in the preheated oven for 10–12 minutes, or until the mushrooms are tender and the stuffing is crisp on the top. Serve garnished with basil sprigs.

Leek & Goat Cheese Tarts

Serve these delicious, easy-to-prepare tarts with an arugula salad as a sit-down appetizer, or on their own as part of a buffet meal.

SERVES 6	PREP 15 MINS	COOK 20 MINS

1 sheet ready-to-bake puff pastry, thawed if frozen

3 tablespoons butter

12 ounces baby leeks, thickly sliced diagonally

1 tablespoon chopped fresh oregano

4 ounces goat cheese, sliced or crumbled

1 tablespoon milk, for brushing

salt and pepper (optional)

1. Preheat the oven to 425°F. Cut the sheet of pastry into six 5-inch squares.

2. Place the pastry squares on a baking sheet and use the tip of a sharp knife to score each one all around about ½-inch from the edge.

3. Melt the butter in a skillet, add the leeks, and sauté gently, stirring frequently, for 4–5 minutes, until soft. Add the oregano, season with salt and pepper, if using, and divide the leek mixture among the pastry squares, placing it inside the scored lines.

4. Top each tart with cheese and brush the pastry with milk. Bake in the preheated oven for 12–15 minutes, until risen and golden brown. Serve warm.

Baked Figs with Gorgonzola

Made with baby figs, just-melting Gorgonzola, delicate wildflower honey, and crisp toast, this appetizer is quite heavenly.

SERVES 4   PREP 15 MINS   COOK 10 MINS

½ loaf French bread (about 4 ounces), sliced into eight ¾-inch-thick slices

8 small fresh figs

2 ounces Gorgonzola cheese, rind removed, cut into 8 squares

4 teaspoons honey

1. Preheat the oven to 350°F. Lightly toast the bread on both sides, then transfer to a small baking sheet.

2. Cut a cross in the top of each fig, lightly press a cube of cheese into each one, then place a fig on top of each slice of toast. Bake in the preheated oven for 5–6 minutes, until the figs are hot and the cheese is just melting.

3. Transfer to a plate. Drizzle with honey and serve immediately.

Tip ALTHOUGH GORGONZOLA IS RENOWNED IN ITALY AS THE TRADITIONAL CULINARY COMPANION FOR SWEET AND JUICY FIGS, YOU CAN USE ANY BLUE CHEESE FOR THIS DISH, EVEN ROQUEFORT OR STILTON, IF YOU WANT TO GIVE IT A REAL TOUCH OF AN OLD WORLD TRADITIONAL CHRISTMAS.

1

2

2

The Main Event

* * * * *

Traditional Roasted Chicken

If you don't have a big crowd for Christmas dinner, a large chicken, cooked and served in the same way, is a good alternative to turkey.

....
SERVES 6   PREP 20 MINS   COOK 1 HR 45 MINS
....

large 5-pound chicken

4 tablespoons butter

2 tablespoons chopped fresh lemon thyme

1 lemon, quartered

½ cup white wine

salt and pepper (optional)

fresh thyme sprigs, to garnish

1. Preheat the oven to 425°F. Make sure the chicken is clean, wiping it inside and out with paper towels, and put it into a roasting pan. Put the butter into a bowl and soften with a fork, then mix in the chopped thyme and season with salt and pepper, if using. Spread the herb butter all over the chicken, inside and out, and put the lemon quarters inside the body cavity. Pour the wine over the chicken.

2. Roast the bird in the center of the preheated oven for 20 minutes. Reduce the oven temperature to 375°F and roast for an additional 1¼ hours, basting frequently. Cover with aluminum foil if the skin begins to brown too much. If the pan dries out, add a little more wine or water.

3. The chicken is ready when a meat thermometer inserted in the thickest part of the meat—in the thigh area near the breast—reads 180°F. Alternatively, test that the chicken is cooked by piercing the thickest part of the leg with a sharp knife and making sure the juices run clear and there is no sign of pink. Remove from the oven. Transfer the chicken to a warm serving plate, cover loosely with foil, and let rest for 10 minutes before carving.

4. Place the roasting pan on the top of the stove and simmer the pan juices gently over low heat until they have reduced and are thick and glossy. Season with salt and pepper, if using. Serve the chicken with the pan juices, garnished with thyme sprigs.

Prime Rib of Beef au Jus

Prime rib of beef is just right for a special meal and is a good option for those who prefer red meat to white for their Christmas feast.

SERVES 8   PREP 10 MINS. PLUS STANDING   COOK 1 HR 40 MINS–2 HRS 25 MINS

6-pound rib of beef
4 tablespoons butter, softened
1½ teaspoons sea salt flakes
1 tablespoon pepper
2 tablespoons flour
4 cups beef broth
freshly cooked vegetables and
roasted potatoes, to serve

1. Place the beef, bone side down, in a deep roasting pan. Rub the entire surface of the meat with the butter and coat evenly with the salt and pepper.

2. Let the beef stand for 1 hour to reach room temperature. Preheat the oven to 450°F. Put the beef into the preheated oven and roast, uncovered, for 20 minutes to sear the outside of the meat.

3. Reduce the oven temperature to 325°F and roast for 15 minutes per 1 pound of meat for medium rare (plus or minus 15 minutes for well done and rare, respectively). Transfer the meat to a large plate and cover with aluminum foil. Let rest for 30 minutes before serving.

4. Meanwhile, pour off all but 2 tablespoons of the fat from the pan and place the pan over medium heat. Add the flour and simmer, stirring with a wooden spoon, for 1 minute, until a thick paste forms. Pour in a ladleful of broth and bring to a boil, then beat into the paste, scraping all the caramelized drippings from the bottom of the pan until smooth. Repeat with the remaining broth, a ladleful at a time.

5. Simmer for 10 minutes, until reduced and slightly thickened. Strain the sauce and keep warm.

6. Cut the beef free from the bone and carve thinly. Serve the jus alongside the carved beef, accompanied by vegetables and roasted potatoes.

Roasted Venison with Brandy Sauce

Saddle of venison is a delicious and seasonal choice for the festive meal, and the rich and creamy brandy sauce complements it perfectly.

SERVES 6   PREP 10 MINS   COOK 1 HR 55 MINS

⅓ cup vegetable oil

3¾-pound loin of fresh venison, trimmed

salt and pepper (optional)

freshly cooked vegetables, to serve

BRANDY SAUCE

1 tablespoon all-purpose flour

¼ cup vegetable broth

¾ cup brandy

½ cup heavy cream

1. Preheat the oven to 350°F. Heat half the oil in a skillet over high heat.

2. Season the venison with salt and pepper, if using, then add to the pan and cook until sealed and lightly browned all over. Pour the remaining oil into a roasting pan. Add the venison, cover with aluminum foil, and roast in the preheated oven, basting occasionally, for 1½ hours, or until cooked through. Remove from the oven and transfer to a warm serving plate. Cover with foil and set aside.

3. To make the sauce, place the roasting pan on the stove over medium heat, add the flour, and cook for 1 minute. Pour in the broth and heat, stirring to loosen the sediment from the bottom of the pan. Gradually stir in the brandy and bring to a boil, then reduce the heat and simmer, stirring, for 10–15 minutes, until the sauce has thickened a little. Remove from the heat and stir in the cream.

4. Serve the venison with the brandy sauce and a selection of freshly cooked vegetables.

Duck with Red Wine & Blueberry Sauce

Duck breasts are a delicious main dish for a small group. The red wine and blueberry sauce is a wonderfully fresh accompaniment.

SERVES 4   PREP 20 MINS, PLUS MARINATING AND STANDING   COOK 20 MINS

4 duck breasts, skin on

4 garlic cloves, chopped

grated zest and juice of 1 orange

1 tablespoon chopped fresh parsley

salt and pepper (optional)

new potatoes and a selection of green vegetables, to serve

RED WINE & BLUEBERRY SAUCE

1 cup blueberries

1 cup red wine

1 tablespoon red currant jelly or grape jelly

1. Use a sharp knife to make several shallow diagonal cuts in each duck breast. Put the duck into a nonmetallic bowl with the garlic, orange zest and juice, and parsley. Season with salt and pepper, if using, and stir well. Turn the duck in the mixture until thoroughly coated. Cover the bowl with plastic wrap and transfer to the refrigerator to marinate for at least 1 hour.

2. Heat a dry, nonstick skillet over medium heat. Add the duck breasts and cook for 4 minutes, then turn them over and cook for an additional 4 minutes, or to taste. Remove from the heat, cover, and let stand for 5 minutes.

3. Halfway through the cooking time, make the sauce. Put the blueberries, red wine and red currant jelly into a separate saucepan. Bring to a boil. Reduce the heat and simmer for 10 minutes, then remove from the heat.

4. Slice the duck breasts and transfer to warm serving plates. Serve with the sauce poured over the duck and accompanied by new potatoes and green vegetables.

Festive Beef Wellington

This truly magnificent dish is worthy of centerpiece status at the festive meal—to do it justice, buy the best-quality beef you can.

....
SERVES 4   **PREP 30 MINS**   **COOK 1 HOUR 10 MINS**
....

1¾ pounds thick
filet mignon

2 tablespoons butter

2 tablespoons vegetable oil

1 garlic clove, chopped

1 onion, chopped

3 cups thinly sliced
cremini mushrooms

1 tablespoon chopped
fresh sage

1 sheet ready-to-bake
puff pastry, thawed if frozen

1 egg, beaten

salt and pepper (optional)

1. Preheat the oven to 425°F. Put the beef into a roasting pan, spread with the butter, and season to taste with salt and pepper, if using. Roast in the preheated oven for 30 minutes, then remove from the oven. Do not turn off the oven.

2. Meanwhile, heat the oil in a saucepan over medium heat. Add the garlic and onion and sauté, stirring, for 3 minutes. Stir in salt and pepper to taste, if using, the mushrooms, and sage and cook, stirring frequently, for 5 minutes. Remove from the heat.

3. Roll out the pastry into a rectangle large enough to enclose the beef, then place the beef in the center and spread the mushroom mixture over it. Bring the long sides of the pastry together over the beef and seal with beaten egg. Tuck the short ends over, trimming away the excess pastry, and seal. Place on a baking sheet, seam side down, and make two slits in the top. Decorate with pastry shapes made from the scraps and brush with the beaten egg. Bake for 40 minutes. Remove from the oven, cut into thick slices, and serve.

> *Tip* YOU CAN SUBSTITUTE THE MORE USUAL MUSHROOM MIXTURE WITH A DELICIOUS ROASTED GARLIC PASTE. SIMPLY ROAST A WHOLE BULB OF GARLIC IN A HOT OVEN FOR 10 MINUTES, THEN MIX THE FLESH WITH SOME OLIVE OIL, FRESH CHOPPED THYME, AND ROSEMARY AND SPREAD IT OVER THE BEEF.

Roasted Pork Loin

Only the best will do at Christmas, and this joint is superb. Rich, moist meat is served with a crisp and crunchy crackling.

SERVES 6   *PREP 25 MINS, PLUS RESTING*   *COOK 2 HRS 10 MINS*

4-pound flat piece pork loin, backbone removed and rind scored

2½ teaspoons salt

¼ teaspoon pepper

3 garlic cloves, crushed

2 tablespoons chopped fresh rosemary

4 fresh rosemary sprigs

1 cup dry white wine

fresh rosemary sprigs, to garnish

cooked seasonal vegetables, to serve

1. Preheat the oven to 450°F. Put the pork on a work surface, skin side down. Make small slits in the meat all over the surface. Season with ½ teaspoon of the salt and the pepper. Rub the garlic all over the meat surface and sprinkle with the chopped rosemary.

2. Roll up the loin and secure the rosemary sprigs on the outside with fine twine. Make sure that the meat is securely tied. Season the rind with the remaining salt to give a good crackling.

3. Transfer the meat to a roasting pan and roast in the preheated oven for 20 minutes, or until the fat has started to run. Reduce the oven temperature to 375°F and pour half the wine over the meat. Roast for an additional 1 hour 40 minutes, basting the meat occasionally with the pan juices.

4. Remove the meat from the oven and let rest in a warm place for 15 minutes before carving. Remove the twine and the rosemary before cutting into thick slices.

5. Pour off all but 1 tablespoon of the fat from the roasting pan. Add the remaining wine to the juices in the pan and bring to a boil, scraping up and stirring in any sediment from the bottom of the pan. Spoon over the meat and serve immediately with fresh vegetables, garnished with extra sprigs of rosemary.

Glazed Ham

Ham can be served as an accompaniment to the Christmas turkey,
although this delicious meat deserves recognition in its own right.

SERVES 8	PREP 20 MINS	COOK 4 HRS 20 MINS

9-pound country ham

1 apple, cored and chopped

1 onion, chopped

1¼ cups hard apple cider or
apple juice

6 black peppercorns

1 bouquet garni
(sprigs of parsley, thyme,
and bay leaf tied together)

50 cloves

¼ cup raw brown sugar

1. Put the ham into a large saucepan and add enough cold water to cover. Bring to a boil and skim off any foam that rises to the surface. Reduce the heat and simmer for 30 minutes.

2. Drain the ham and return to the pan. Add the apple, onion, cider, peppercorns, bouquet garni, and a few of the cloves. Pour in enough fresh water to cover and bring back to a boil. Cover and simmer for 3 hours 20 minutes.

3. Preheat the oven to 400°F. Take the pan off the heat and set aside to cool slightly. Remove the ham from the cooking liquid and, while it is still warm, loosen the rind with a sharp knife, then peel it off and discard.

4. Score the fat into diamond shapes and stud with the remaining cloves. Place the ham on a rack in a roasting pan and sprinkle with the sugar. Roast in the preheated oven, basting occasionally with the cooking liquid, for 20 minutes. Serve hot or cold.

Poached Salmon

*A whole poached salmon makes an impressive and special main dish
on Christmas Day. Serve with lemon and fresh vegetables.*

SERVES 6   PREP 20 MINS   COOK 6-8 MINS, PLUS STANDING

1 whole 6–8 pound salmon
(head on)

3 tablespoons salt

3 bay leaves

10 black peppercorns

1 onion, peeled and sliced

1 lemon, sliced

lemon wedges, to serve

1. Wipe the salmon thoroughly inside and out with paper towels, then use the back of a chef's knife to remove any scales that might still be on the skin. Remove the fins with a pair of scissors and trim the tail. Some people prefer to cut off the head, but it is traditionally served with it on.

2. Place the salmon on the two-handle rack that comes with a fish poacher, then place it in the poacher. Fill the poacher with enough cold water to cover the salmon adequately. Sprinkle with the salt, bay leaves, and peppercorns and sprinkle in the onion and lemon slices.

3. Place the poacher over low heat, over two burners, and bring just to a boil slowly.

4. Cover and simmer gently. Simmer for 6–8 minutes and let stand in the hot water for 15 minutes before removing. Serve with lemon wedges for squeezing over the fish.

Roasted Monkfish with Scalloped Potatoes

Delicious firm-fleshed monkish is served here with melt-in-the-mouth scalloped potatoes. Add crisp salad greens for a well-rounded plate.

SERVES 4   PREP 20 MINS   COOK 55 MINS–1 HR 10 MINS

3 tablespoons butter, melted

6 red-skinned or white round potatoes (about 1½ pounds), peeled and thinly sliced

1 onion, thinly sliced

1 tablespoon coarsely chopped fresh thyme

1 cup vegetable broth

4 skinless monkfish fillets (about 7 ounces each)

¼ cup olive oil

finely pared zest of 1 lemon

½ cup chopped fresh flat-leaf parsley

1 garlic clove, crushed

salt and pepper (optional)

1. Preheat the oven to 400°F. Brush a shallow ovenproof dish with a little of the melted butter. Layer the potatoes, onion, and thyme in the dish, seasoning well between the layers with salt and pepper, if using, and finishing with a layer of potatoes.

2. Pour in enough of the broth to come halfway up the potatoes and drizzle the remaining melted butter over the top. Bake in the center of the preheated oven for 40–50 minutes, pressing the potatoes into the broth once or twice with the back of a spatula until tender and brown on top.

3. Season the monkfish with salt and pepper, if using. Mix together the oil, lemon zest, parsley, and garlic and rub all over the monkfish. Sear the monkfish in a smoking-hot skillet or on a ridged grill pan for 1 minute on each side, or until browned. Transfer the monkfish to a roasting pan, spaced well apart, and roast on the top shelf of the oven for the final 12–15 minutes of the cooking time, until just cooked through. Serve immediately with the potatoes.

Mixed Nut Roast

This lusciously rich nut roast is a good vegetarian option for an indulgent Christmas dinner and it cooks much more quickly than a turkey or goose.

❧

SERVES 4 · PREP 15 MINS · COOK 35 MINS

1 tablespoon butter,
for greasing

2 tablespoons butter

2 garlic cloves, chopped

1 large onion, chopped

⅓ cup pine nuts, toasted

¾ cup hazelnuts, toasted

½ cup ground walnuts

⅓ cup ground cashew nuts

2 cups fresh whole-wheat
bread crumbs

1 egg, lightly beaten

2 tablespoons chopped
fresh thyme

1 cup vegetable broth

salt and pepper (optional)

fresh thyme sprigs,
to garnish

CRANBERRY &
RED WINE SAUCE

1¾ cups fresh cranberries

½ cup sugar

1¼ cups red wine

1 cinnamon stick

1. Preheat the oven to 350°F. Grease an 8½ x 4½ x 2½-inch loaf pan and line it with wax paper.

2. Melt the butter in a saucepan over medium heat. Add the garlic and onion and cook, stirring, for about 3 minutes. Remove the pan from the heat.

3. Grind the pine nuts and hazelnuts in a mortar with a pestle. Stir into the pan with the walnuts and cashew nuts and add the bread crumbs, egg, thyme, broth, and seasoning, if using.

4. Spoon the mixture into the prepared pan and level the surface. Cook in the center of the preheated oven for 30 minutes or until cooked through and golden and a toothpick inserted into the center of the loaf comes out clean.

5. Halfway through the cooking time, make the sauce. Put the cranberries, sugar, wine, and cinnamon into a saucepan over medium heat and bring to a boil. Reduce the heat and simmer, stirring occasionally, for 15 minutes.

6. Remove the nut roast from the oven and turn out onto a serving plate. Garnish with thyme sprigs and serve.

1

4

5

Roasted Butternut Squash

Butternut squash has a great flavor—stuffed with beans, mushrooms, and zucchini, it makes a substantial vegetarian or vegan main dish.

SERVES 4   PREP 40 MINS, PLUS STANDING   COOK 1 HR 10 MINS

1 small butternut squash

1 onion, chopped

2–3 garlic cloves, crushed

4 small tomatoes, chopped

1⅓ cups chopped cremini mushrooms

¼ cup drained, canned lima beans, rinsed and coarsely chopped

1 zucchini, trimmed and grated

2 tablespoons chopped fresh oregano

2 tablespoons tomato paste

1¼ cups water

4 scallions, trimmed and chopped

1 tablespoon vegetarian Worcestershire sauce

pepper (optional)

1. Preheat the oven to 375°F. Prick the squash all over with the tip of a sharp knife, then roast in the preheated oven for 40 minutes, or until tender. Remove from the oven and let stand until cool enough to handle. Do not turn off the oven.

2. Cut the squash in half, scoop out and discard the seeds, then scoop out some of the flesh, making hollows in both halves. Chop the scooped-out flesh and put into a bowl. Place the two squash halves side by side in a large roasting pan.

3. Add the onion, garlic, tomatoes, and mushrooms to the squash flesh in the bowl. Add the beans, zucchini, half the oregano, and pepper, if using, and mix well together. Spoon the filling into the two halves of the squash, packing it down as firmly as possible.

4. Mix the tomato paste with the water, scallions, and Worcestershire sauce in a small bowl and pour around the squash.

5. Cover loosely with a large sheet of aluminum foil and bake for 30 minutes, or until piping hot. Serve in warm bowls, garnished with the remaining oregano.

1

3

4

Roasted Beet Packages with Polenta

Beets with horseradish is an amazing combination, the wonderful sweet earthiness of the beets complemented by the bite of the horseradish.

SERVES 4   **PREP 20 MINS, PLUS COOLING**   **COOK 2 HRS**

2 tablespoons olive oil, for greasing and tossing

8 small beets, peeled and halved

4 fresh thyme sprigs

¼ cup grated fresh horseradish, or grated horseradish from a jar

1 stick unsalted butter

salt and pepper (optional)

arugula, to serve

POLENTA

3¾ cups water

1¼ cups quick-cooking polenta or grits

1 teaspoon salt

1. To make the polenta, bring the water to a boil in a large saucepan. Slowly add the polenta and salt, stirring constantly. Simmer, stirring frequently, for 30–40 minutes, until the mixture comes away from the side of the pan.

2. Grease a small roasting pan. Transfer the polenta to the pan, level the surface, and let cool.

3. Preheat the oven to 375°F. Toss the beets with enough oil to coat.

4. Place four beet halves and a thyme sprig on a square of thick aluminum foil. Season with salt and pepper, if using. Wrap in a loose package, sealing the edges. Repeat with the remaining beet halves to make four packages in total. Roasted in the preheated oven for 1 hour, or until just tender.

5. Meanwhile, mash the horseradish with the butter and a little salt and pepper, if using. Roll into a log, using a piece of plastic wrap, seal, and chill in the refrigerator.

6. Preheat the broiler to high. Slice the polenta into four neat rectangles. Spread out in a broiler pan, brush with oil, and cook under a hot broiler for 5 minutes. Turn and broil for an additional 3 minutes, until crisp.

7. Arrange the polenta on serving plates. Place the beets and a slice of horseradish butter on top and serve with arugula.

Superb Sides & Sauces

✳ ✳ ✳ ✳ ✳ ✳

Perfect Roasted Potatoes

With a crisp, golden crust and steaming hot and fluffy white flesh, roasted potatoes are the ideal accompaniment to a traditional Christmas dinner.

SERVES 8	PREP 25 MINS	COOK 1 HR 25 MINS

⅓ cup goose fat

1 teaspoon coarse sea salt

18 small russet potatoes
of an equal size or
2¼ pounds new potatoes

fresh rosemary sprigs,
to garnish

1. Preheat the oven to 450°F. Put the fat into a large roasting pan, sprinkle generously with the salt, and place in the preheated oven.

2. Meanwhile, bring a large saucepan of water to a boil, add the potatoes, bring back to a boil, and cook for 8–10 minutes, until parboiled. Drain well and, if the potatoes are large, cut them in half. Return the potatoes to the empty pan and shake vigorously to roughen them on the outside.

3. Arrange the potatoes in a single layer in the hot fat and roast in the preheated oven for 45 minutes. If they look as if they are beginning to char around the edges, reduce the oven temperature to 400°F. Turn the potatoes over and roast for an additional 30 minutes, until crisp. Garnish with rosemary sprigs and serve immediately.

Tip

TOSS THE PARBOILED POTATOES IN
A LITTLE DRY ENGLISH MUSTARD TO
CREATE AN EXTRA-GOLDEN CRUST.
IF YOU CAN'T GET GOOSE FAT, USE THE
SAME QUANTITY OF DUCK FAT OR
OLIVE OIL INSTEAD.

Mashed Sweet Potatoes

This tasty mash is a delicious accompaniment to any roasted meat, and its wonderful bright color will enhance the Christmas dining table.

SERVES 4	PREP 10 MINS	COOK 25 MINS, PLUS STANDING

5 tablespoons butter, softened

2 tablespoons chopped fresh parsley

6 sweet potatoes (about 2 pounds), scrubbed

1. Reserving 2 tablespoons, put the butter into a bowl with the parsley and beat together. Turn out onto a square of aluminum foil or plastic wrap, shape into a block, and transfer to the refrigerator to chill until required.

2. Cut the sweet potatoes into even chunks. Bring a large saucepan of water to a boil, add the sweet potatoes, bring back to a boil, and cook, covered, for 15–20 minutes, until tender.

3. Drain the potatoes well, then cover the pan with a clean dish towel and let stand for 2 minutes. Remove the skins and mash with a potato masher until fluffy.

4. Add the reserved butter to the potatoes and stir in evenly. Spoon the mash into a serving dish and serve hot, topped with chunks of parsley butter.

1

3

3

Braised Red Cabbage

Slow-cooked, lightly spiced red cabbage is the ideal accompaniment to rich meat dishes, such as pork, goose, game, or even sausages.

SERVES 4	PREP 15 MINS	COOK 50–55 MINS

2 tablespoons butter

1 large red onion, thinly sliced

1 small red cabbage, outer leaves removed

⅓ cup vegetable broth

¼ teaspoon ground cinnamon

5 juniper berries, lightly crushed

finely grated zest and juice of ½ orange

2 teaspoons packed light brown sugar

4–5 firm ripe plums, pitted and halved or quartered if large

salt and pepper (optional)

1. Melt the butter in a saucepan. Add the onion, cover, and sauté gently for 5 minutes, until soft. Meanwhile, quarter and core the cabbage and shred finely.

2. Add the cabbage to the pan with the broth, cinnamon, juniper berries, orange zest and juice, and sugar. Mix well. Cover and cook over low heat for 35 minutes.

3. Stir in the plums and season with salt and pepper, if using. Cover and cook for an additional 10–12 minutes, until tender. Serve immediately.

Variation REPLACE THE PLUMS WITH A PEELED, CORED, AND CHOPPED COOKING APPLE, SUCH AS GRANNY SMITH, ADDING IT WITH THE CABBAGE. A LITTLE RED WINE VINEGAR, STIRRED IN WITH THE ORANGE ZEST AND JUICE, WILL BRING OUT ALL THE OTHER FLAVORS AND ADD EXTRA BITE.

Sugar-Glazed Parsnips

Parsnips are a vastly underrated vegetable, whose inherent sweetness is emphasized with the addition of a deliciously sticky sugar glaze.

SERVES 8   PREP 5 MINS   COOK 50 MINS

24 small parsnips
1 teaspoon salt
1 stick butter
½ cup firmly packed light brown sugar

1. Put the parsnips into a saucepan, add just enough water to cover, then add the salt. Bring to a boil, reduce the heat, cover, and simmer for 20–25 minutes, until tender. Drain well.

2. Melt the butter in a heavy skillet or wok. Add the parsnips and toss well. Sprinkle with the sugar, then cook, stirring frequently to prevent the sugar from sticking to the pan or burning, for 10–15 minutes, until golden and glazed. Transfer to a warm serving dish and serve immediately.

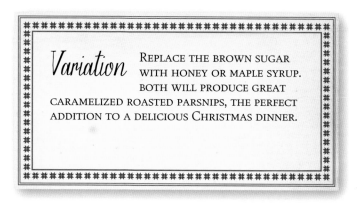

Variation REPLACE THE BROWN SUGAR WITH HONEY OR MAPLE SYRUP. BOTH WILL PRODUCE GREAT CARAMELIZED ROASTED PARSNIPS, THE PERFECT ADDITION TO A DELICIOUS CHRISTMAS DINNER.

Sticky Carrots with Whiskey & Ginger Glaze

Sweet carrots are given added zing with a spicy whiskey glaze, making them a worthy accompaniment to the Christmas roasted meats.

| SERVES 2–3 | PREP 15 MINS | COOK 20 MINS |

1 teaspoon sugar

½ teaspoon pepper

good pinch of sea salt flakes

¼ cup peanut oil

3 tablespoons salted butter

4 large carrots, sliced diagonally into ½-inch circles

¾-inch piece fresh ginger, cut into sticks

2 tablespoons whiskey

½ cup chicken broth

1. Mix the sugar, pepper ,and salt together in a bowl and set aside until needed.

2. Heat the oil with half the butter in a large skillet. Add the carrots in a single layer and sprinkle with the sugar mixture. Cook over medium–high heat for 3 minutes, then start turning the slices with tongs and reduce the heat, if necessary. When brown on both sides and starting to blacken at the edges, transfer to a plate.

3. Wipe out the pan with paper towels. Add the ginger and cook over medium-high heat for 1–2 minutes, until golden. Add to the carrots.

4. Add the remaining butter, the whiskey, and broth. Bring to a boil, then reduce the heat and simmer for 3 minutes or until syrupy. Return the carrots and ginger to the pan and swirl with the syrup for 1 minute. Serve immediately.

Pecan-Glazed Brussels Sprouts

Perfectly cooked nutty-flavored Brussels sprouts are given some extra festive crunch with the addition of golden toasted pecans.

SERVES 6	PREP 15 MINS	COOK 35 MINS

1½ pounds Brussels sprouts
½ cup water
4 tablespoons unsalted butter
⅓ cup firmly packed light brown sugar
3 tablespoons soy sauce
¼ teaspoon salt
½ cup finely chopped pecans, toasted

1. Cut off the stem ends of the sprouts and slash the bottom of each sprout with a shallow "X." Bring the water to a boil in a large saucepan; add the sprouts, cover, then reduce the heat and simmer for 8–10 minutes, or until the sprouts are slightly softened, then drain and set aside.

2. Melt the butter in a skillet and stir in the sugar, soy sauce, and salt. Bring to a boil, stirring constantly. Add the nuts, reduce the heat, and simmer, uncovered, for 5 minutes, stirring occasionally. Add the sprouts and cook over medium heat for 5 minutes. Stir well before serving.

❄ Variation ❄

FOR A MORE TRADITIONAL FINISH TO THIS DISH, YOU COULD SUBSTITUTE THE PECANS WITH CHOPPED OR SLIVERED BLANCHED ALMONDS.

Cranberry Sauce

Succulent and zingy cranberry sauce is the perfect accompaniment to roasted turkey—and you can use any leftovers in the turkey sandwiches.

SERVES 8	PREP 20 MINS	COOK 5 MINS

thinly pared zest and juice of 1 lemon

thinly pared zest and juice of 1 orange

3½ cups cranberries, thawed if frozen

¾ cup sugar

2 tablespoons arrowroot, mixed with 3 tablespoons cold water

1. Put the lemon zest and orange zest into a heavy saucepan. Add the cranberries, lemon juice, orange juice, and sugar to the pan and cook over medium heat, stirring occasionally, for 5 minutes, or until the berries begin to burst.

2. Strain the juice into a clean saucepan and reserve the cranberries. Stir the arrowroot mixture into the juice, then bring to a boil, stirring constantly, until smooth and thick. Remove from the heat and stir in the reserved cranberries.

3. Transfer the cranberry sauce to a bowl and let cool, then cover with plastic wrap and chill in the refrigerator until ready to use.

Garlic Mushrooms with Chestnuts

That all-time favorite, garlic mushrooms, is given a festive twist with the addition of chestnuts, cream, and a splash of white wine.

....
| SERVES 4 | PREP 15 MINS | COOK 15 MINS |
....

4 tablespoons butter

4 garlic cloves, chopped

3 cups sliced button mushrooms

3 cups sliced cremini mushrooms

¼ cup dry white wine

½ cup heavy cream

1 (10-ounce) can whole chestnuts, drained

4 ounces chanterelle mushrooms, sliced

salt and pepper (optional)

chopped fresh parsley, to garnish

1. Melt the butter in a large saucepan over medium heat. Add the garlic and cook, stirring, for 3 minutes, until soft. Add the button mushrooms and cremini mushrooms and cook for 3 minutes.

2. Stir in the wine and cream and season with salt and pepper, if using. Cook for 2 minutes, stirring, then add the chestnuts and the chanterelle mushrooms. Cook for an additional 2 minutes, stirring, then remove from the heat and transfer to a warm serving dish. Garnish with chopped fresh parsley and serve.

Rich Onion Gravy

The secret to well-flavored gravy is to use a really good-quality broth—homemade if possible.

| SERVES 8 | PREP 15 MINS | COOK 1 HR 25 MINS |

2 tablespoons sunflower oil

4 onions (about 1 pound), thinly sliced

2 garlic cloves, crushed

1 tablespoon sugar

3 tablespoons all-purpose flour

⅔ cup red wine

2½ cups boiling beef broth

2 teaspoons Dijon mustard

salt and pepper (optional)

1. Heat the oil in a large, heavy saucepan. Add the onions, garlic, and sugar and sauté over low heat for 30 minutes, stirring occasionally, until soft and light golden brown.

2. Stir in the flour and cook for 1 minute. Add the wine and bring to a boil, then simmer and beat until the mixture is smooth. Add ⅔ cup of the broth and bring back to a boil. Simmer and beat again to mix thoroughly.

3. Stir in the remaining broth and the mustard. Bring back to a boil and season with salt and pepper, if using.

4. Simmer for 20 minutes and serve immediately.

Mango & Macadamia Stuffing

Much of the appeal of the Christmas turkey is the stuffing, for which there are many variations. The exotic flavors make this one special.

SERVES 4–6   *PREP 10 MINS*   *COOK 30 MINS*

---

1 tablespoon butter, for greasing

2 tablespoons butter

1 small onion, finely chopped

1 celery stalk, diced

4 cups fresh white bread crumbs

1 egg, beaten

1 tablespoon Dijon mustard

1 small mango, peeled, pitted, and diced

½ cup chopped macadamia nuts

salt and pepper (optional)

1. Preheat the oven to 400°F. Grease a 3-cup ovenproof dish.

2. Melt the butter in a saucepan, add the onion, and sauté, stirring, for 3–4 minutes, until soft. Add the celery and cook for an additional 2 minutes.

3. Remove from the heat and stir in the bread crumbs, egg, and mustard. Add the mango and nuts, then season to taste with salt and pepper, if using.

4. Spread the mixture in the prepared dish and bake in the preheated oven for 20–25 minutes, until golden and bubbling. Serve hot.

Tip YOU CAN USE SOME OF THE MIXTURE TO STUFF THE NECK END OF THE BIRD BEFORE ROASTING, AND BAKE THE REMAINDER OF THE STUFFING ACCORDING TO THE RECIPE, OR YOU CAN ROLL IT INTO WALNUT-SIZE BALLS AND BAKE IT IN THE OVEN FOR 15–20 MINUTES.

Divine Desserts

✳ ✳ ✳ ✳ ✳

Cheesecake with Caramel Pecans

This delicious baked cheesecake, with its lovely caramelized pecan decoration, is a dessert worthy of gracing the Christmas table.

SERVES 6–8   PREP 25 MINS   COOK 1 HR 20 MINS–1 HR 30 MINS

CRUST

½ cup pecans

22 graham crackers
(about 5½ ounces),
broken into pieces

4 tablespoons butter, melted

FILLING

1¾ cups cream cheese

1 cup ricotta cheese

½ cup superfine or
granulated sugar

3 extra-large eggs

3 extra-large egg yolks

1 cup heavy cream

TOPPING

1 tablespoon butter,
for greasing

1 cup superfine or
granulated sugar

⅓ cup water

¾ cup pecan halves

1. Preheat the oven to 325°F. To make the crust, put the nuts into a food processor and process briefly, then add the broken cookies and pulse again until crumbs form. Transfer to a bowl and stir in the melted butter until well combined. Press into the bottom of an 8-inch round springform cake pan. Bake in the preheated oven for 10 minutes, then remove from the oven and let cool.

2. To make the filling, beat together the cream cheese, ricotta cheese, and sugar in a large bowl. Beat in the eggs and egg yolks, one at a time, until smooth. Finally, stir in the cream. Spoon over the prepared crust. Bake in the preheated oven for 1 hour, then test; the cheesecake should be cooked but have a slight "wobble" in the center. Return to the oven for an additional 10 minutes, if necessary. Remove from the oven and let cool in the pan.

3. To make the topping, grease a piece of aluminum foil with butter and lay it flat. Put the sugar and water into a saucepan and heat gently, stirring, until the sugar has dissolved. Bring to a simmer, swirling the saucepan instead of stirring, and cook until the syrup begins to darken, then add the pecans. Transfer each nut to the greased foil and let harden. When you are ready to serve, unmold the cheesecake onto a serving plate and arrange the caramel pecans on top.

1

2

3

Apple Pie

This classic dessert is perfect to round off Christmas dinner.
Add more cinnamon to the filling if you're feeling extra-festive.

SERVES 6–8   PREP 40 MINS, PLUS CHILLING   COOK 50 MINS

1⅓ cups all-purpose flour
pinch of salt
6 tablespoons butter,
cut into pieces
⅓ cup lard, cut into small
pieces
1–2 tablespoons water
1 egg, beaten, for glazing
1 tablespoon light brown
sugar, for sprinkling

FILLING
6 cooking apples,
such as Granny Smiths
(about 2 pounds), peeled,
cored, and sliced
½ cup firmly packed
light brown sugar
½–1 teaspoon ground
cinnamon

1. Sift the flour and salt into a mixing bowl. Add the butter and lard and rub in with your fingertips until the mixture resembles fine bread crumbs. Add enough cold water to mix to a firm dough. Wrap in plastic wrap and chill for 30 minutes.

2. Preheat the oven to 425°F. Thinly roll out almost two-thirds of the dough and use to line a deep 9-inch pie plate.

3. To make the filling, mix the apples with the sugar and cinnamon and pack into the pastry shell.

4. Roll out the remaining dough to make a lid. Dampen the edges of the pastry rim with water and position the lid, pressing the edges firmly together. Trim and crimp the edges. Use the dough scraps to cut out leaves or other shapes. Dampen and attach to the top of the pie. Glaze the pie with beaten egg, make one or two slits in the top, and place the pie on a baking sheet.

5. Bake in the preheated oven for 20 minutes, then reduce the temperature to 350°F and bake for an additional 30 minutes, or until the pastry is a light golden brown. Sprinkle with sugar and serve hot or cold.

Prosecco
& Lemon Sorbet

This deliciously light and refreshing dessert is a delight after a heavy meal—or you could serve it as a palate cleanser between courses.

SERVES 4   PREP 10 MINS. PLUS COOLING AND FREEZING   COOK 5 MINS

¾ cup superfine or
granulated sugar

½ cup water

finely grated zest and juice
of 1 lemon

1½ cups prosecco

fresh mint sprigs, to decorate

1. Put the sugar, water, and lemon zest into a medium-size saucepan over low heat and heat, stirring constantly, until the sugar is dissolved.

2. Bring to a boil, then boil for 1 minute until slightly reduced. Let cool, then strain through a sieve.

3. Add the lemon juice and prosecco to the lemon syrup and stir to combine, then pour into an ice-cream machine and churn following the manufacturer's directions. Alternatively, pour into a container to freeze and whisk once an hour until completely frozen.

4. Remove the sorbet from the freezer about 15 minutes before serving, then scoop into serving dishes. Decorate with mint sprigs and serve.

Cranberry Amaretti Creams

All the lovely flavors of Christmas—ginger, cinnamon, and tart, juicy cranberries—come together in this luscious and creamy cold dessert.

SERVES 10　　　　PREP 15 MINS, PLUS COOLING AND CHILLING　　　　COOK 10 MINS

⅓ cup granulated sugar

2 teaspoons cornstarch

large pinch of ground cinnamon

large pinch of ground ginger

½ cup water

2 cups frozen cranberries

⅔ cup cream cheese

3 tablespoons superfine sugar

1 cup heavy cream

4 teaspoons orange juice

12 amaretti cookies, crushed

1. Put the granulated sugar, cornstarch, cinnamon, and ginger into a heavy saucepan, then gradually add the water, stirring, until smooth. Add the cranberries and cook for 5–8 minutes, stirring occasionally, until they are soft and the mixture has thickened. Cover and let cool.

2. Put the cheese and superfine sugar into a mixing bowl and stir, then gradually whisk in the cream until smooth. Stir in the orange juice and then the cookie crumbs. Spoon the mixture into a disposable paper or plastic pastry bag. Spoon the cranberry mixture into a separate disposable pastry bag. Snip off the tips.

3. Pipe the amaretti cream into ten shot glasses until they are one-quarter full. Pipe half the cranberry mixture over the top, then repeat the layers. Cover and chill.

Pear & Ginger Bundt Cakes

Bundt cakes have become a traditional Christmas offering, and these miniature versions, with their luscious whiskey glaze, are irresistible.

SERVES 12   PREP 20 MINS   COOK 35–40 MINS

½ tablespoon butter,
for greasing

1 tablespoon flour, for dusting

1 large or 2 small pears,
peeled, cored, and cubed

1 tablespoon packed
dark brown sugar

1 stick butter, softened

¾ cup plus 2 tablespoons
superfine or granulated sugar

2 eggs, beaten

½ cup sour cream

1⅓ cups all-purpose flour,
sifted

1 teaspoon baking powder

1 teaspoon ground ginger

pinch of salt

¼ cup finely chopped
crystallized ginger

2 teaspoon vanilla extract

GLAZE

2 tablespoons whiskey

¼ cup firmly packed
dark brown sugar

1. Preheat the oven to 350°F. Grease a 12-cup mini Bundt pan and lightly dust with flour, shaking out any excess.

2. Put the pears into a small saucepan with a splash of cold water and the brown sugar. Cook over low heat for 3–4 minutes, until the pears are soft but not mushy. Drain through a strainer, reserving the cooking juices, and let cool.

3. Put the butter and superfine sugar into a mixing bowl and beat until light and fluffy. Gradually beat in the eggs, adding a spoonful of the flour if the mixture curdles. Stir in the sour cream.

4. Mix the flour with the baking powder, ground ginger, salt, and 2 tablespoons of the crystallized ginger, then gently fold into the mixture with the vanilla extract and the pears.

5. Spoon the batter into the prepared pan and bake in the preheated oven for 25–30 minutes, until risen and golden. Let cool in the pan for a few minutes, then transfer to a wire rack to cool completely.

6. To make the glaze, place the reserved cooking juices in a small saucepan with the whiskey and sugar, bring to a boil, and boil hard for 2–3 minutes, until slightly reduced and thickened. Spoon over the tops of the cakes and sprinkle with the remaining crystallized ginger.

Cranberry Apple Meringues

Apples cooked until tender with zesty dried cranberries, then covered with a soft meringue topping—it all adds up to a delicious dessert.

SERVES 4	*PREP 10 MINS*	*COOK 25–30 MINS*

3 cooking apples, such as Granny Smiths (about 1 pound)

1 tablespoon apple juice

¾ cup plus 2 tablespoons superfine sugar

¾ cup dried cranberries

2 egg whites

1. Preheat the oven to 400°F. Peel, core, and chop the apples, put into a saucepan, and sprinkle with the apple juice.

2. Add ⅓ cup of the sugar and the cranberries, stir, and heat gently until boiling. Cover the pan, reduce the heat, and simmer gently, stirring occasionally, for 8–10 minutes, until the fruit is just tender.

3. Divide the fruit among four 1½-cup ovenproof dishes and place on a baking sheet.

4. Put the egg whites into a grease-free bowl and whisk until they hold soft peaks. Gradually whisk in the remaining sugar until the mixture holds stiff peaks.

5. Spoon the meringue on top of the fruit, swirling with a knife. Bake in the preheated oven for 10–12 minutes, until the meringue is lightly browned. Serve warm.

Tip

THIS IS A GOOD DINNER-PARTY DESSERT, BECAUSE IT'S REALLY EASY TO PREPARE IN ADVANCE. JUST COOK THE APPLE MIXTURE AND SET ASIDE UNTIL NEEDED, THEN REHEAT AND PROCEED WITH THE RECIPE FROM STEP 3.

Poached Pears

Pears poached in red wine make an elegant dessert—and they are an excellent standby, because they can be prepared well in advance.

SERVES 6   PREP 20 MINS, PLUS CHILLING AND COOLING   COOK 50 MINS–1 HR 5 MINS

6 Bosc pears, peeled but left whole with stems attached

2 cups medium red wine

½ cup water

1 tablespoon packed light brown sugar

1 piece of lemon zest or tangerine zest

1 vanilla bean

1½ cups heavy cream

1 tablespoon confectioners' sugar

1. Put the pears into a large saucepan with the red wine, water, brown sugar, and lemon zest and gently bring to a boil, stirring to make sure that the sugar has dissolved. Reduce the heat, cover, and simmer for 30 minutes, until the pears are tender. Let the pears cool in the liquid, then remove from the liquid, cover, and chill in the refrigerator.

2. Discard the lemon zest and simmer the liquid for 15–20 minutes, or until syrupy. Let cool.

3. Cut a thin sliver of flesh from the bottom of each pear so that they will stand upright. Slice open the vanilla bean lengthwise and scrape out the seeds into a bowl. Add the cream and confectioners' sugar to the vanilla seeds and whisk together until thick. Put each pear onto a dessert plate and pour over a little syrup. Serve with the vanilla cream.

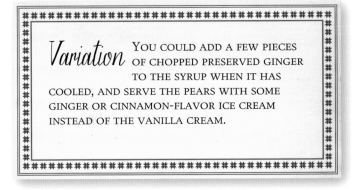

Variation YOU COULD ADD A FEW PIECES OF CHOPPED PRESERVED GINGER TO THE SYRUP WHEN IT HAS COOLED, AND SERVE THE PEARS WITH SOME GINGER OR CINNAMON-FLAVOR ICE CREAM INSTEAD OF THE VANILLA CREAM.

Mango & Ginger Roulade

Mango and ginger are brought together in a delicious combination for this delicious dessert, which is perfect for entertaining.

SERVES 6   PREP 30 MINS   COOK 15–20 MINS

1 tablespoon oil, for oiling

1 tablespoon superfine or granulated sugar, for sprinkling

1¼ cups all-purpose flour

1½ teaspoons baking powder

1½ sticks butter, softened

¾ cup plus 2 tablespoons superfine or granulated sugar

3 eggs, beaten

1 teaspoon vanilla extract

2 tablespoons orange juice

1 large ripe mango

3 tablespoons chopped candied ginger

⅓ cup crème fraîche or mascarpone cheese

1. Preheat the oven to 350°F. Grease a 9 x 13-inch cake pan and line with parchment paper, leaving an overhang of ½ inch above the rim. Lay a sheet of parchment paper on the work surface and sprinkle with the superfine sugar.

2. Sift the flour and baking powder into a large bowl and add the butter, sugar, eggs, and vanilla extract. Beat well until smooth, then beat in the orange juice. Spoon the batter into the prepared pan and smooth into the corners with a spatula. Bake in the preheated oven for 15–20 minutes, or until risen, firm, and golden brown.

3. Meanwhile, peel and pit the mango and cut into chunks. Reserve a few pieces for decoration and finely chop the remainder. Transfer to a small bowl and stir in 2 tablespoons of the candied ginger.

4. Turn out the cake onto the prepared paper and spread with the mango mixture. Firmly roll up the cake from one short side to enclose the filling, keeping the paper around the outside to hold it in place. Carefully transfer to a wire rack to cool, removing the paper when firm.

5. When cold, top with spoonfuls of crème fraîche and decorate with the reserved mango and the remaining candied ginger.

Chocolate Mousse

This simplest of desserts is one of the most satisfying. To get the best flavor, make sure you use the best dark chocolate.

SERVES 4–6   PREP 10 MINS, PLUS CHILLING   COOK 6–10 MINS

10 ounces semisweet chocolate, broken into small pieces

1½ tablespoons unsalted butter

1 tablespoon brandy

4 eggs, separated

2 ounces semisweet chocolate, broken into small pieces, to serve

1. Put the chocolate and butter into a heatproof bowl set over a saucepan of gently simmering water and heat, stirring, until smooth. Remove from the heat, stir in the brandy, and let cool slightly. Add the egg yolks and beat until smooth.

2. In a separate bowl, whisk the egg whites until they hold stiff peaks, then fold into the chocolate mixture. Spoon into small serving bowls or glasses and level the surfaces. Transfer to the refrigerator and chill for 4 hours, or until set.

3. Take the mousse out of the refrigerator and serve, sprinkled with chopped chocolate pieces.

1

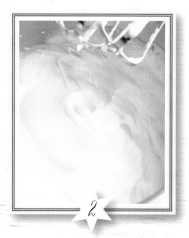

2

2

Rich Chocolate Pies

Chocolate and cream, baked together in a rich and delicious pie—what could be better as a dessert during the indulgent festive season?

SERVES 8   PREP 20 MINS, PLUS CHILLING   COOK 35 MINS

PASTRY DOUGH

1¾ cups all-purpose flour

1 stick butter, diced

2 tablespoons confectioners' sugar

1 egg yolk

2–3 tablespoons cold water

1 tablespoon flour, for dusting

FILLING

8 ounces semisweet chocolate, broken into pieces

1 stick butter

⅓ cup confectioners' sugar

1¼ cups heavy cream

grated chocolate, to decorate

1. To make the pastry dough, sift the flour into a large bowl. Add the butter and rub it in with your fingertips until the mixture resembles bread crumbs. Add the confectioners' sugar, egg yolk, and enough water to form a soft dough. Wrap the dough in plastic wrap and chill in the refrigerator for 15 minutes. Roll out the dough on a lightly floured surface and use to line eight 4-inch shallow tart pans. Chill for 30 minutes.

2. Preheat the oven to 400°F. Prick the pastry shells with a fork and line with crumpled aluminum foil. Bake in the preheated oven for 10 minutes, then remove the foil and bake for an additional 5–10 minutes. Transfer to a wire rack to cool. Reduce the oven temperature to 325°F.

3. To make the filling, put the chocolate, butter, and confectioners' sugar into a heatproof bowl set over a saucepan of gently simmering water and heat until melted. Remove from the heat and stir in 1 cup of the cream. Remove the pastry shells from the pans and place on a baking sheet. Fill each case with some of the chocolate mixture. Return to the oven and bake for 5 minutes. Remove from the oven and let cool, then chill until required.

4. Whip the remaining cream and pipe into the center of each tart. Decorate with grated chocolate and serve.

Yuletide Baking

* * * * * *

Christmas Tree Wreath Cake

Celebrate the festive season with this delightful themed cake—with the added surprise of a green Christmas tree running through the middle.

SERVES 16   PREP 60 MINS. PLUS CHILLING   COOK 1 HR 55 MINS. PLUS COOLING

GREEN CAKE

½ tablespoon butter,
for greasing

1 tablespoon flour, for dusting

1¾ cups all-purpose flour

2 teaspoons baking powder

2 sticks butter, softened

1 cup plus 2 tablespoons
superfine or granulated sugar

4 extra-large eggs

green food coloring paste

VANILLA CAKE

2 cups all-purpose flour

2 teaspoons baking powder

2 sticks butter, softened

2 cups plus 2 tablespoons
superfine or granulated sugar

4 extra-large eggs

1 teaspoon vanilla extract

TO DECORATE

2 cups store-bought
vanilla buttercream

2 teaspoon mixed red,
white, and green confetti
sugar sprinkles

1 teaspoon silver candied balls

1. Preheat the oven to 325°F. Thoroughly grease a 2-quart tube cake pan, then lightly dust with flour.

2. To make the green cake, put the all-purpose flour, baking powder, butter, sugar, and eggs into a large bowl and beat with a handheld electric mixer for 1–2 minutes, until smooth and creamy. Beat in enough food coloring to give the batter a Christmas tree-green color.

3. Spoon the batter into the prepared pan and level the surface. Bake in the preheated oven for 45–50 minutes, or until risen, firm to the touch, and a toothpick inserted into the middle of the cake comes out clean. Let cool in the pan for 10 minutes, then turn out carefully onto a wire rack and let cool completely. Turn off the oven.

4. Place the cold cake on a board and use a sharp knife to cut it into 16 wedge-shape slices. Slightly separate the slices (still maintaining the ring shape), then chill in the freezer for 30 minutes.

5. Use a Christmas tree-shape cookie cutter to stamp out 16 Christmas tree shapes from the chilled cake wedges. Reform the trees into the ring shape again and return to the freezer for an additional 30–40 minutes, or until firm.

6. Meanwhile, preheat the oven to 325°F. Clean the pan, then grease it and lightly dust with flour.

7. To make the vanilla cake, put all the ingredients into a large bowl and beat with a handheld electric mixer for 1–2 minutes, until smooth and creamy. Spoon the batter into a pastry bag fitted with a plain tip.

8. Pipe three lines of batter into the bottom of the prepared pan, then continue piping the batter up the side of the pan and smooth with a spatula to cover the bottom and sides completely.

9. Take two Christmas tree cake shapes together and gently place in the vanilla batter, pointed side down and leaning into the center of the pan. Repeat with the remaining slices, keeping them as close together as possible to reform the ring shape (upside down) inside the pan.

10. Pipe the remaining vanilla batter around the other sides of the trees and over the tops to cover them completely. Gently level the surface.

11. Bake in the preheated oven for 45 minutes, then loosely cover the top of the cake with aluminum foil. Bake for an additional 15–20 minutes, or until a toothpick inserted into the cake comes out clean (make sure to put the toothpick into an area where there is more vanilla cake). Let cool in the pan for 15 minutes. Run a small angled spatula around the side of the cake, carefully turn out onto a wire rack, and let cool completely.

12. To decorate, spread some of the buttercream in a thin layer all over the cake. Chill the cake in the refrigerator for 30 minutes. Spread the remaining buttercream all over the cake, swirling it with a spatula. Decorate with confetti sprinkles and silver candied balls.

Dark Chocolate Yule Log

This chocolate delight is the traditional French and Belgian Christmas cake—when you've sampled it, you'll see why it's so popular.

SERVES 8   PREP 45 MINS, PLUS COOLING   COOK 20 MINS

½ tablespoons butter, for greasing

1 tablespoon flour, for dusting

1 tablespoon superfine sugar, for sprinkling

¾ cup superfine or granulated sugar

4 eggs, separated

1 teaspoon almond extract

1 cup all-purpose flour

1 teaspoon baking powder

10 ounces semisweet chocolate, broken into pieces

1 cup heavy cream

2 tablespoons rum

holly sprig, to decorate

1 tablespoon confectioners' sugar, for dusting

1. Preheat the oven to 375°F. Grease a 16 x 11-inch baking pan, line with parchment paper, then dust with flour. Sprinkle a sheet of wax paper with superfine sugar.

2. Reserving 2 tablespoons, put the superfine sugar into a bowl with the egg yolks and beat until thick and pale. Stir in the almond extract. Whisk the egg whites in a separate bowl until they hold soft peaks. Gradually beat in the reserved sugar until the mixture is stiff and glossy.

3. Sift half the flour and baking powder into the egg yolk mixture and fold in, then fold in one-quarter of the egg white. Sift and fold in the remaining flour and baking powder, followed by the remaining egg whites. Spoon the batter into the prepared pan, spreading it evenly with a spatula. Bake in the preheated oven for 15 minutes, until lightly golden. Turn out onto the prepared paper, then roll up and let cool.

4. Put the chocolate into a heatproof bowl. Bring the cream to boiling point in a small saucepan, then pour it over the chocolate and stir until the chocolate has melted. Beat until smooth and thick. Reserve about one-third of the chocolate mixture and stir the rum into the remainder. Unroll the cake and spread with the chocolate-and-rum mixture. Reroll and place on a large plate or cake board. Evenly spread the reserved chocolate mixture over the top and side of the cake. Mark with a fork so that the surface resembles tree bark. Just before serving, decorate with a holly sprig and sprinkle with confectioners' sugar to resemble snow.

Festive Cupcakes

These delicately decorated, mixed fruit and orange cupcakes will take pride of place on your table.

MAKES 14   PREP 20 MINS, PLUS COOLING   COOK 15–20 MINS

⅔ cup mixed dried fruit

1 teaspoon finely grated orange zest

2 tablespoons brandy or orange juice

6 tablespoons butter, softened

⅓ cup firmly packed light brown sugar

1 extra-large egg, lightly beaten

1 cup all-purpose flour

1 teaspoon baking powder

1 teaspoon allspice

1 tablespoon silver candied balls, to decorate

ICING

⅔ cup confectioners' sugar

2 tablespoons orange juice

1. Put the mixed fruit, orange zest, and brandy into a small bowl. Cover and let soak for 1 hour.

2. Preheat the oven to 375°F. Put 14 paper cupcake liners into two cupcake pans or put 14 double-layer paper liners on a baking sheet.

3. Put the butter and sugar into a mixing bowl and beat together until light and fluffy. Gradually beat in the egg. Sift in the flour, baking powder, and allspice and, using a metal spoon, fold them into the mixture, followed by the soaked fruit. Spoon the batter into paper liners.

4. Bake the cupcakes in the oven for 15–20 minutes or until golden brown and firm to the touch. Transfer to a cooling rack and let cool.

5. To make the icing, sift the confectioners' sugar into a bowl and gradually mix in enough orange juice until the mixture is smooth and thick enough to coat the back of a wooden spoon. Using a teaspoon, drizzle the icing in a zigzag pattern over the cupcakes. Decorate with the silver candied balls and let set.

Holly Cupcakes

These picture-perfect cupcakes are quick to make and easy to decorate—and they will certainly impress your guests.

MAKES 16   PREP 45 MINS, PLUS COOLING   COOK 20 MINS

1 stick butter, softened

1 cup superfine or granulated sugar

4 eggs, lightly beaten

a few drops of almond extract

1¼ cups all-purpose flour

1¼ teaspoons baking powder

1¾ cups ground almonds

1 pound white ready-to-use fondant

1 tablespoon confectioners' sugar, for dusting

2 ounces green ready-to-use fondant

1 ounce red ready-to-use fondant

1. Preheat the oven to 350°F. Line two 8-cup cupcake pans with paper cupcake liners.

2. Put the butter and superfine sugar into a large bowl and beat together until light and fluffy. Gradually beat in the eggs and almond extract. Sift in the flour and baking powder and, using a metal spoon, fold into the mixture with the ground almonds.

3. Spoon the batter into the paper liners. Bake in the preheated oven for 20 minutes, or until the cupcakes are risen, golden, and firm to the touch. Transfer to a wire rack and let cool completely.

4. Roll out the white fondant to a thickness of ¼ inch on a surface lightly dusted with confectioners' sugar. Using a 2¾-inch plain cutter, stamp out 16 circles, rerolling the fondant as necessary. Place a circle on top of each cupcake.

5. Roll out the green fondant to the same thickness. Using a holly cutter, cut out 32 leaves, rerolling the fondant as necessary. Brush each leaf with a little water and place two leaves on top of each cupcake. Roll tiny balls from the red fondant to make 48 small berries and place on the leaves.

135

Apple & Cinnamon Bran Muffins

These delicious, gluten-free muffins are so delicious that you will want to make them all year round.

¼ cup vegetable oil

1 tablespoon food-grade glycerin (available from cake supply stores or online)

¾ cup applesauce

2 eggs

½ teaspoon vanilla extract

¼ cup honey

⅓ cup milk

about 2 cups gluten-free all-purpose flour

1¼ cups gluten-free oat bran

⅔ cup ground flaxseed

1 teaspoon gluten-free baking powder

½ teaspoon gluten-free baking soda

½ teaspoon xanthan gum

1 teaspoon cinnamon

¼ teaspoon allspice

¾ cup firmly packed light brown sugar

⅓ cup raisins

⅓ cup golden raisins

1. Preheat the oven to 350°F. Line a 12-cup muffin pan with decorative paper muffin cups.

2. In a large bowl, whisk together the oil, glycerin, applesauce, eggs, vanilla extract, honey, and milk. In a separate bowl, mix all the remaining ingredients together, then add the liquid mixture and stir well. If the batter seems too wet, add a little more gluten-free flour.

3. Divide the batter among the paper cups. Bake the muffins in the preheated oven for 20–25 minutes, or until a toothpick inserted into the center of a muffin comes out clean. Remove from the oven and let cool on a wire rack.

Tip IF YOU PREFER, YOU COULD ADD SOME CHOPPED ALMONDS, HAZELNUTS, WALNUTS, PECANS, OR MACADAMIA NUTS TO THE DRY INGREDIENTS TO GIVE THE MUFFINS A LITTLE CRUNCH AND EXTRA FLAVOR.

Christmas Macarons

With their Christmas-flavored filling and sparkling gold decoration, these delicious mouthfuls will certainly enhance the festivities.

¾ cup ground almonds

1 cup confectioners' sugar

1 teaspoon ground allspice

2 extra-large egg whites

¼ cup superfine sugar

½ teaspoon freshly grated nutmeg

1 teaspoon gold candied balls

FILLING

4 tablespoons unsalted butter, softened

juice and finely grated zest of ½ orange

1 teaspoon ground allspice

1 cup confectioners' sugar, sifted

2 tablespoons finely chopped candied cherries

1. Put the ground almonds, confectioners' sugar, and allspice into the bowl of a food processor and process for 15 seconds. Sift the mixture into a bowl. Line two baking sheets with parchment paper.

2. Put the egg whites into a large bowl and whisk until they hold soft peaks. Gradually whisk in the superfine sugar to make a firm, glossy meringue. Using a spatula, fold the almond mixture into the meringue, one-third at a time. When all the dry ingredients are thoroughly incorporated, continue to cut and fold the mixture until it forms a shiny batter with a thick, ribbon-like consistency.

3. Pour the batter into a pastry bag fitted with a ½-inch plain tip. Pipe 32 small circles onto the prepared baking sheets. Tap the baking sheets firmly on a work surface to remove air bubbles. Sprinkle half the macarons with the grated nutmeg and gold candied balls. Let stand at room temperature for 30 minutes. Meanwhile, preheat the oven to 325°F.

4. Bake the macarons in the oven for 10–15 minutes. Let cool for 10 minutes, then carefully peel the macarons off the paper. Transfer to a wire rack and let cool completely.

5. To make the filling, beat the butter in a bowl with the orange juice and zest until fluffy. Gradually beat in the allspice and confectioners' sugar until smooth and creamy. Fold in the candied cherries and use the mixture to sandwich pairs of macarons together.

1

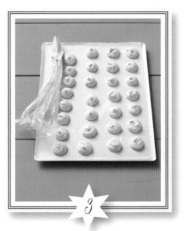

3

5

Christmas Cranberry & Orange Pies

If you're a lover of cranberry sauce, you'll be delighted with these delicious little fruit pies, filled with the taste of Christmas.

MAKES 12   PREP 15 MINS, PLUS COOLING   COOK 30 MINS

½ tablespoon butter,
for greasing

2 cups frozen cranberries

1 tablespoon cornstarch

3 tablespoons freshly squeezed
orange juice

2 star anise

¼ cup granulated sugar

1 sheet store-bought rolled
dough pie crust, chilled

1 tablespoon all-purpose
flour, for dusting

1 tablespoon milk,
for brushing

1 tablespoon sugar,
for sprinkling

1. Preheat the oven to 350°F. Lightly grease a 12-cup mini muffin pan. Put the cranberries into a saucepan with the cornstarch and orange juice. Add the star anise and cook over low heat, stirring occasionally, for 5 minutes, or until the cranberries are soft. Add the sugar and cook for an additional 5 minutes, then remove from the heat and let cool.

2. Thinly roll out the dough on a lightly floured surface. Using a fluted cookie cutter, stamp out twelve 2½-inch circles and gently press them into the prepared pan, reserving the scraps. Brush the top edges of the pastry shells with a little milk. Remove and discard the star anise, then spoon in the filling.

3. Thinly roll out the dough scraps. Using a fluted pastry wheel, cut out thin strips of dough. Arrange these over each pie in a lattice pattern, brush with milk, and sprinkle with sugar. Bake in the preheated oven for 20 minutes. Let cool in the pan for 10 minutes, then transfer to a wire rack. Serve warm or cold.

Christmas Tree Cookies

If you like to make your own Christmas decorations, you'll love these—but don't be surprised if they mysteriously disappear from the tree.

MAKES 12   PREP 20 MINS. PLUS CHILLING AND COOLING   COOK 10–12 MINS

1¼ cups all-purpose flour

1 teaspoon ground cinnamon

½ teaspoon freshly grated nutmeg

½ teaspoon ground ginger

5 tablespoons unsalted butter, diced

3 tablespoons honey

1 tablespoon butter, for greasing

1 tablespoon all-purpose flour, for dusting

white icing and silver candied balls (optional) and narrow ribbon, to decorate

1. Sift the flour and spices into a bowl and rub in the butter until the mixture resembles bread crumbs. Add the honey and mix well together to form a soft dough. Halve the dough, shape into balls, wrap in plastic wrap, and chill in the refrigerator for 30 minutes.

2. Preheat the oven to 350°F and lightly grease two baking sheets. Roll out one piece of dough on a floured work surface to thickness of ¼ inch. Cut out tree shapes using a cutter. Repeat with the remaining dough.

3. Put the cookies onto the prepared baking sheets and, using a toothpick, make a hole through the top of each cookie large enough to thread the ribbon through. Chill in the refrigerator for 15 minutes.

4. Bake in the preheated oven for 10–12 minutes, until golden. Let cool on the baking sheets for 5 minutes, then transfer to a wire rack to cool completely. Decorate the trees with icing and silver candied balls, or leave them plain. Thread the ribbon through the cookies and hang them on the Christmas tree.

141

Rudolph Cookies

Everyone loves a Christmas-themed cookie, and these reindeer ones are sure to be a favorite with children and adults alike.

MAKES 16　　　PREP 30 MINS, PLUS CHILLING AND COOLING　　　COOK 15–18 MINS

1 stick unsalted butter, softened

½ cup superfine or granulated sugar

1 medium egg

1⅓ cups all-purpose flour

1¼ teaspoons baking powder

ICING

¾ cup confectioners' sugar

2–3 teaspoons cold water

TO DECORATE

small pretzels

red candies

chocolate sprinkles

1. Put the butter into a large bowl and beat with a handheld electric mixer until soft. Add the superfine sugar, egg, flour and baking powder and beat well to make a smooth dough. Wrap in plastic wrap and chill in the refrigerator for 10 minutes. Line two baking sheets with parchment paper.

2. Unwrap the dough and divide into 16 pieces, rolling with your hands into slightly oval balls. Place on the prepared baking sheets, spaced well apart to allow for spreading.

3. Carefully slice off the top of each pretzel with a serrated knife. Press two pretzels into the top of each cookie for antlers. Chill in the refrigerator for 10 minutes. Meanwhile, preheat the oven to 350°F.

4. Bake in the preheated oven for 15–18 minutes, until just golden. Let cool on the baking sheets for a few minutes, then transfer to wire racks to cool completely.

5. To make the icing, sift the confectioners' sugar into a bowl and gradually add the water, stirring to a thick, toothpastelike consistency. Spoon into a squeeze bottle.

6. Pipe a dab of icing in the center of each cookie and press on a red candy for the nose. Pipe two small dabs of icing for eyes and top each with a chocolate sprinkle. Let dry.

1

3

6

Mini Gingerbread House Cookies

Have fun decorating each of these mini gingerbread houses differently. Color the royal icing with food coloring and use different candies.

1 stick butter

2 tablespoons light corn syrup

¾ cup firmly packed
light brown sugar

2⅓ cups all-purpose flour

2¼ teaspoons baking powder

2 teaspoons ground ginger

1 extra-large egg, beaten

ROYAL ICING

1¼ cups confectioners' sugar

2 teaspoons
dried egg white powder

2 tablespoons cold water

TO DECORATE

red and green candies

1. Put the butter and light corn syrup into a saucepan and heat gently, stirring, until melted. Remove the pan from the heat and stir in the sugar until dissolved.

2. Sift the flour, baking powder, and ginger into a large bowl and make a well in the center with a wooden spoon. Pour in the warm ingredients and the beaten egg and stir until a smooth dough forms. Wrap the dough in plastic wrap and chill in the refrigerator for about 20 minutes, or until just firm. Line two baking sheets with parchment paper.

3. Unwrap the dough and place between two large sheets of parchment paper. Roll out to an even thickness of ¼ inch. Use a knife to cut the dough into twenty-four 2¾-inch squares. Cut 8 squares in half diagonally to make 16 triangles.

4. Carefully transfer the remaining squares to the prepared baking sheets. Place a triangle next to each square, with the long side touching one side of the square to make a roof for the house. Chill in the refrigerator for 10 minutes. Meanwhile, preheat the oven to 325°F.

5. Bake the cookies in the preheated oven for 12–15 minutes, until firm and lightly browned. Let cool on the baking sheets for a few minutes, then transfer to wire racks to cool completely.

6. To make the royal icing, sift the confectioners' sugar into a large bowl and add the egg white powder and water. Stir with a spoon until smooth, then use an electric handheld mixer to beat the icing for 3–4 minutes, until it is thick, like toothpaste.

7. Spoon the royal icing into a pastry bag fitted with a No. 2 tip. Pipe a line of icing around the roof of each cookie and pipe roof tiles, if desired. Add a front door and windows. Pipe jagged lines under the roofs and on the ground for icicles and snow. Decorate with red and green candies. Let the icing set.

Get in the Spirit

* * * * * *

Holiday Eggnog

This sweet and creamy drink has a welcome hit of brandy and a touch of rum for that winter-warming effect on a cold day.

SERVES 9   PREP 10 MINS, PLUS CHILLING   COOK 25 MINS

---

6 extra-large eggs

½ cup superfine sugar,
plus 2 tablespoons extra

2 cups light cream

2 cups milk

½ cup brandy

¼ cup light rum

1 teaspoon vanilla extract

2 cups heavy cream

freshly grated nutmeg,
to decorate

1. Whisk the eggs with a handheld electric mixer on medium speed until thick and lemon in color, then gradually add the ½ cup of sugar, whisking well.

2. Put the light cream and milk into a large saucepan over medium–low heat and heat until hot but not boiling. Gradually add the hot milk mixture to the egg mixture, stirring with a wire whisk. Return the mixture to the pan and cook over medium-low heat, stirring constantly with a wire whisk until hot but not boiling. Remove from the heat and let cool. Stir in the brandy, rum, and vanilla extract with a wire whisk. Cover and chill in the refrigerator until thoroughly chilled.

3. Just before serving, whip the heavy cream with the remaining sugar in a large bowl until it holds soft peaks. Pour the chilled eggnog mixture into a large punch bowl. Gently fold the whipped cream into the eggnog mixture just until combined. Decorate with freshly grated nutmeg.

Mulled Ale &
Mulled Wine

These classic recipes have really stood the test of time. Apart from tasting delicious, they will fill your kitchen with warm and spicy aromas.

MAKES 3 QUARTS — PREP 20 MINS, PLUS STANDING — COOK 35 MINS

MULLED ALE

10½ cups premium ale

1¼ cups brandy

2 tablespoons sugar

large pinch of ground cloves

large pinch of ground ginger

MULLED WINE

5 oranges

50 cloves

thinly pared zest and
juice of 4 lemons

3½ cups water

½ cup sugar

2 cinnamon sticks

3 (750-milliliter) bottles
red wine

⅔ cup brandy

1. To make the mulled ale, put all the ingredients into a heavy saucepan and heat gently, stirring, until the sugar has dissolved. Continue to heat so that it is simmering but not boiling. Remove the saucepan from the heat and serve the ale immediately in heatproof glasses.

2. To make the mulled wine, prick the skins of three of the oranges all over with a fork and stud with the cloves, then set aside. Thinly pare the zest and squeeze the juice from the remaining oranges.

3. Put the orange zest and juice, lemon zest and juice, water, sugar, and cinnamon in a heavy saucepan and bring to a boil over medium heat, stirring occasionally, until the sugar has dissolved. Boil for 2 minutes without stirring, then remove from the heat, stir once, and let stand for 10 minutes. Strain the liquid into a heatproof bowl.

4. Pour the wine into a separate saucepan and add the strained spiced juices, the brandy, and the clove-studded oranges. Simmer gently without boiling, then remove from the heat. Strain into heatproof glasses and serve immediately.

Kir Royale

A truly luxurious drink for a festive cocktail party. The addition of a little brandy gives this innocent-tasting cocktail a kick.

SERVES 1	PREP 2 MINS	COOK NONE

few drops crème de cassis, or to taste
2 tablespoons brandy
champagne, chilled
fresh mint spring, to decorate

1. Put the cassis into the bottom of a champagne flute.

2. Add the brandy. Top up with champagne.

3. Garnish with the mint sprig and serve immediately.

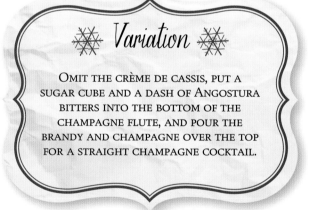

❄ Variation ❄

OMIT THE CRÈME DE CASSIS, PUT A SUGAR CUBE AND A DASH OF ANGOSTURA BITTERS INTO THE BOTTOM OF THE CHAMPAGNE FLUTE, AND POUR THE BRANDY AND CHAMPAGNE OVER THE TOP FOR A STRAIGHT CHAMPAGNE COCKTAIL.

Mimosa

The perfect cocktail for an extra-special Christmas brunch. Bright and fresh-tasting, this classic drink will have you celebrating in style.

SERVES 1	PREP 2 MINS	COOK NONE

2 measures chilled fresh orange juice

2 measures champagne, chilled

1. Fill a chilled flute halfway with orange juice.

2. Gently pour in the chilled champagne.

3. Serve immediately.

❋ Variation ❋

MAKE A PITCHER OF MIMOSA SO THAT YOUR GUESTS CAN SERVE THEMSELVES, LEAVING YOU FREE TO PREPARE THE REST OF THE FOOD. MAKE SURE YOU KEEP THE RATIO OF HALF CHAMPAGNE AND HALF ORANGE JUICE THE SAME.

Hot Brandy Chocolate

The natural affinity between brandy and chocolate is well demonstrated here. Whipped cream adds that extra touch of Christmas indulgence.

SERVES 4　　　PREP 5 MINS　　　COOK 20 MINS

4 cups milk

4 ounces chocolate, broken into pieces

2 tablespoons sugar

½ cup brandy

⅓ cup whipped cream

freshly grated nutmeg, for sprinkling

1. Heat the milk in a small saucepan to just below boiling.

2. Add the chocolate and sugar and stir over low heat until the chocolate has melted.

3. Pour into four warm heatproof glasses, then carefully pour 2 tablespoons of the brandy over the back of a spoon into each glass.

4. Add the whipped cream and sprinkle with the grated nutmeg. Serve immediately.

1

2

3

Midnight's Kiss

Drink it at midnight, or at any other time—this flute of clear sapphire loveliness will add glamour and sparkle to any party.

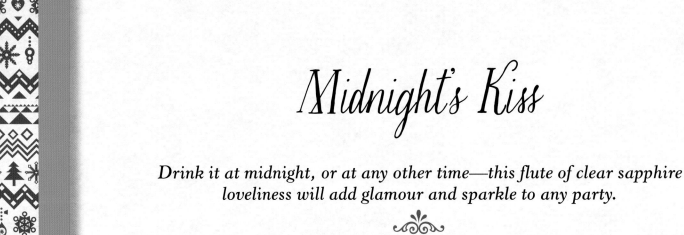

SERVES 1 · PREP 5 MINS · COOK NONE

sugar
wedge of lemon
1 tablespoon vodka
2 teaspoons blue curaçao
cracked ice
sparkling wine

1. Spread out the sugar on a plate. Run a wedge of lemon around the rim of a chilled champagne flute to moisten it, and then dip the glass into the sugar.

2. Add the vodka and curaçao to a shaker filled with ice.

3. Shake well, strain into the glass, and top up with sparkling wine. Serve immediately.

Tip

YOU CAN USE ANY SUGAR FOR RIMMING THE GLASS—OR BUY GOLD SUGAR FROM A SPECIALTY SUPPLIER TO INCREASE THE GLAMOUR FACTOR OF THIS COCKTAIL.

Stuffed Olives

Olives are a traditional standby canapé, and it's always useful to have a jar on hand—the delicious stuffings in these make them really delectable.

❦

SERVES 6   PREP 20 MINS   COOK NONE

¼ cup Spanish extra virgin olive oil

1 tablespoon sherry vinegar, or to taste

2 tablespoons finely chopped parsley

finely grated zest of ½ orange

18 large pitted ripe black olives

18 large pitted green olives

12 anchovy fillets in oil, drained

½ roasted red bell pepper in oil, drained and cut into 12 small pieces

12 blanched almonds

1. Whisk together the oil, vinegar, parsley, and orange zest in a small serving bowl, adding extra vinegar to taste. Set aside until needed.

2. Make a lengthwise slit in 12 of the black olives and 12 of the green olives without cutting all the way through.

3. Roll up the anchovy fillets and gently press them into the cavities of six of the slit green olives and six of the slit black olives.

4. Use the pieces of roasted red pepper to stuff the remaining slit olives. Slip a blanched almond into the center of each of the remaining olives.

5. Add all the olives to the bowl of dressing and stir gently. Serve with wooden toothpicks for spearing the olives.

Stuffed Mini Bell Peppers

Filled with oozing cheese, these tasty little morsels are perfect for serving as canapés for a seasonal drinks party.

SERVES 12   PREP 30–35 MINS   COOK 15 MINS

1 tablespoon olive oil, for oiling

⅓ cup cream cheese

2 garlic cloves, finely chopped

2 teaspoons finely chopped fresh rosemary

1 tablespoon finely chopped fresh basil

1 tablespoon finely chopped fresh parsley

3 tablespoons finely grated Parmesan cheese

1 cup finely chopped cooked chicken breast

3 scallions, finely chopped

12 mixed baby bell peppers, (about 12 ounces)

salt and pepper (optional)

1. Preheat the oven to 375°F. Lightly brush a large baking sheet with oil.

2. Put the cream cheese, garlic, rosemary, basil, and parsley into a bowl, then add the Parmesan cheese and stir together, using a metal spoon.

3. Mix in the chicken and scallions, then season with a little salt and pepper, if using.

4. Slit each bell pepper from the tip up to the stem, leaving the stem in place, then make a small cut just to the side, so that you can get a teaspoon into the center of the pepper to scoop out the seeds.

5. Fill each bell pepper with some of the chicken mixture, then place on the prepared baking sheet. Cook in the preheated oven for 15 minutes, or until the peppers are soft and light brown in patches.

6. Let cool slightly on the baking sheet, then transfer to a serving plate. Serve warm or cold. These are best eaten on the day they are made and should be kept in the refrigerator if serving cold.

Mini Turkey Pies with Cranberry Relish

These mini turkey pies will carry the traditional taste of Christmas through to any evening get-together after the big day.

SERVES 12   PREP 20 MINS, PLUS COOLING   COOK 33–35 MINS

1 sheet store-bought rolled
dough pie crust, chilled

1 tablespoon all-purpose
flour, for dusting

1 egg yolk mixed with
1 tablespoon water,
for glazing

12 ounces ground turkey

4 scallions, finely chopped

2 garlic cloves, finely chopped

leaves from 4 fresh
thyme sprigs

1 teaspoon ground allspice

2 egg yolks

salt and cayenne pepper
(optional)

CRANBERRY RELISH

1 tablespoon olive oil

1 red onion, thinly sliced

1 cup frozen cranberries

3 tablespoons cranberry sauce

¼ cup ruby port or red wine

1. Preheat the oven to 350°F. Line a 12-cup muffin pan with squares of nonstick parchment paper.

2. Thinly roll out the dough on a lightly floured surface. Using a 5-inch plain round cutter, stamp out 12 circles. Press these gently into the prepared pan, so the dough stands just above the top of the pan in soft pleats, rerolling the scraps as needed. Brush the top edges of the pastry shells with a little of the egg glaze.

3. Put the turkey, scallions, garlic, and thyme leaves into a mixing bowl. Sprinkle with the allspice and a little salt and cayenne pepper, if using, then stir in the egg yolks until well mixed. Spoon the filling into the pastry shells and press the tops flat with the back of a teaspoon.

4. Bake in the preheated oven for 30 minutes, or until the pastry is golden and the filling is cooked through. Let cool in the pans for 5 minutes, then loosen with a blunt knife and transfer to a wire rack until needed.

5. Meanwhile, to make the relish, heat the oil in a skillet, add the onion, and sauté until just beginning to soften. Add the remaining ingredients and cook for 3–4 minutes, or until the cranberries are soft. Spoon over the top of the baked pies and serve.

Blinis with Shrimp & Wasabi Cream

These unusual and delicious little canapés couldn't be more dainty—and they could certainly grace the most elegant of cocktail parties.

SERVES 6   PREP 30 MINS, PLUS CHILLING AND STANDING   COOK 10–15 MINS

2¾ cups all-purpose flour

1 cup buckwheat flour

2 teaspoons active dry yeast

2½ cups milk, warmed

6 eggs, separated

3 tablespoons unsalted butter, melted

⅓ cup sour cream

¼ cup clarified butter

WASABI CREAM

1 cup sour cream or crème fraîche

½ teaspoon wasabi paste, or to taste

salt (optional)

TO SERVE

10 ounces cooked shrimp, peeled and deveined

3 tablespoons thinly sliced pickled ginger

2 tablespoons fresh cilantro leaves

1. Sift together the all-purpose flour and buckwheat flour into a large bowl and stir in the yeast. Make a hollow in the center and add the milk, then gradually beat in the flour until you have a smooth batter. Cover and chill in the refrigerator overnight.

2. Two hours before you need the blinis, remove the batter from the refrigerator and let stand for 1 hour 20 minutes to return to room temperature. Beat in the egg yolks, melted butter, and sour cream. In a separate bowl, whisk the egg whites until stiff, then gradually fold into the batter. Cover and let rest for 30 minutes.

3. Meanwhile, make the wasabi cream. Mix together the sour cream and wasabi paste in a small bowl until combined. Taste and add a little more wasabi paste, if you prefer it hotter. Season to taste with salt, if using, then cover and chill in the refrigerator.

4. To cook the blinis, heat a little of the clarified butter in a nonstick skillet over medium–high heat. When hot and sizzling, drop in 3–4 tablespoons of the batter, spaced well apart, and cook until puffed up and tiny bubbles appear around the edges. Flip them over and cook for another few minutes on the other side. Remove from the pan and keep warm while you cook the remaining batter.

5. To serve, spoon a little of the wasabi cream onto a blini, add 1–2 shrimp and a few slices of pickled ginger, then sprinkle with a few cilantro leaves.

Mozzarella Crostini with Pesto & Caviar

These traditional Italian appetizers are given the festive touch when cut into the familiar symbols of a traditional Christmas.

	SERVES 4	PREP 25 MINS	COOK 15 MINS

8 slices white bread, crusts removed

3 tablespoons olive oil

8 ounces firm mozzarella cheese, diced

⅓ cup lumpfish roe

PESTO

2 cups finely chopped fresh basil

¼ cup finely chopped pine nuts

2 garlic cloves, finely chopped

3 tablespoons olive oil

1. Preheat the oven to 350°F. Using a sharp knife, cut the bread into fancy shapes, such as crescent moons, stars, and Christmas trees. Drizzle with the oil, transfer to an ovenproof dish, and bake in the preheated oven for 15 minutes.

2. While the bread is baking, make the pesto. Put the basil, pine nuts, and garlic into a small bowl. Pour in the oil and stir well to combine.

3. Remove the bread shapes from the oven and let cool. Spread a layer of pesto on all of the shapes, top each one with a piece of mozzarella cheese and some lumpfish roe, and serve immediately.

Bruschetta with Fava Beans & Goat Cheese

A wonderful summer flavor served as a vegetarian appetizer at a winter party—feta cheese is a tasty alternative to the goat cheese.

SERVES 6	PREP 30 MINS	COOK 25 MINS

4 cups shelled small fava beans

3 tablespoons extra virgin olive oil

1 tablespoon lemon juice

1 tablespoon chopped fresh mint leaves

6 slices ciabatta

1 large garlic clove, halved

1 teaspoon extra virgin olive oil, for drizzling

⅓ cup fresh vegetarian goat cheese

sea salt flakes and pepper (optional)

1. Bring a large saucepan of water to a boil. Add the beans, bring back to a boil, and cook for 3 minutes, until just tender. Rinse under cold running water and drain. Slip off the bean skins and discard.

2. Toss the beans with the oil, lemon juice, and most of the mint. Season with a little salt and pepper, if using.

3. Transfer the bean mixture to a food processor. Process briefly to a chunky puree.

4. Toast the bread on both sides. While the bread is still warm, rub one side of each slice with the cut garlic clove. Drizzle with oil.

5. Cut each bread slice in half. Spread with the bean mixture, top with goat cheese, and serve immediately.

Lovely Leftovers

✳ ✳ ✳ ✳ ✳

Turkey Club Sandwiches

These sandwiches solve the perennial problem of what to do with all that leftover turkey—homemade mayonnaise is the making of them.

❦

SERVES 6   PREP 30 MINS   COOK 10 MINS

12 pancetta slices
18 slices white bread
12 cooked turkey breast slices
3 plum tomatoes, sliced
6 butterhead lettuce leaves
6 stuffed olives
salt and pepper (optional)

MAYONNAISE
2 extra-large egg yolks
1 teaspoon dry English mustard
1 teaspoon salt
1¼ cups peanut oil
1 teaspoon white wine vinegar

1. First, make the mayonnaise. Put the egg yolks into a bowl, add the dry mustard, pepper, if using, and salt, then beat together well. Pour the oil into a liquid measuring cup with a spout. Begin to whisk the egg yolks, adding just a drop of the oil. Make sure that it has been thoroughly absorbed before adding another drop and whisking well.

2. Continue adding the oil, a drop at a time, until the mixture thickens and stiffens; at this point, whisk in the vinegar and then continue to dribble in the remaining oil slowly in a thin stream, whisking constantly, until all the oil has been used and you have a thick mayonnaise. Cover and refrigerate while you prepare the other sandwich components.

3. Broil or fry the pancetta until crisp, drain on paper towels, and keep warm. Toast the bread until golden, then cut off the crusts. You will need three slices of toast for each sandwich. For each sandwich, spread the first piece of toast with a generous amount of mayonnaise, top with two slices of turkey, keeping the edges tidy, and then top with a couple of slices of tomato. Season to taste with salt and pepper, if using. Add another slice of toast and top with two pancetta slices and one lettuce leaf. Season to taste again, add a little more mayonnaise, then top with the final piece of toast. Push a toothpick through a stuffed olive, and then push it through the sandwich to hold it together.

Chicken & Dumplings

This classic dish comes together in a flash when you use leftover roasted chicken, and it's just right for a warming meal on a cold day.

....

| SERVES 4 | PREP 20 MINS | COOK 35 MINS |

....

2 tablespoons olive oil

1 large onion

2 celery stalks

2 carrots

1 tablespoon fresh thyme leaves

1 teaspoon salt

½ teaspoon pepper

4 tablespoons butter

½ cup all-purpose flour

2 tablespoons milk

6 cups chicken broth

3 cups bite-size, cold roasted chicken pieces

1 cup frozen peas

2 tablespoons fresh parsley leaves, to garnish

DUMPLINGS

2 tablespoons butter

½ cup fresh chives

2 cups all-purpose flour

2 teaspoons baking powder

¾ teaspoon salt

1 cup milk

1. Heat the oil in a large, heavy saucepan over medium-high heat. Dice the onion, celery, and carrots and add them to the pan. Cook, stirring, for about 3 minutes, until the onion is translucent. Add the thyme, salt, and pepper and cook for an additional minute. Add the butter and heat until melted, then stir the flour into the butter. Cook until the butter and flour have browned. Stir in the milk and add the broth. Bring to a boil, then reduce the heat to medium and simmer for about 10 minutes. Meanwhile, shred the chicken.

2. To make the dumplings, put the butter into a microwave-safe dish. Cover the dish and cook on Low for 30 seconds, or until melted. Snip the chives. Put the flour, baking powder, and salt into a bowl and stir to combine. Stir in the butter, milk and chives until just combined.

3. Stir the chicken and peas into the stew, then drop small spoonfuls of the dumpling batter on top. Cover and simmer for 12–15 minutes, until the dumplings are cooked through. Meanwhile, finely chop the parsley. Ladle the stew and dumplings into warm bowls. Garnish with parsley and serve immediately.

Turkey Soup with Rice, Mushrooms & Sage

This delicious soup makes good use of the leftover turkey and the broth you've made from the carcass, although chicken broth will do just as well.

SERVES 4–5   PREP 20 MINS   COOK 1 HR

3 tablespoons butter

1 onion, finely chopped

1 celery stalk, finely chopped

25 large fresh sage leaves, finely chopped

¼ cup all-purpose flour

5 cups turkey broth

½ cup brown rice

3½ cups sliced button mushrooms

1½ cups diced cooked turkey

1 cup heavy cream

salt and pepper (optional)

sprigs of fresh sage, to garnish

freshly grated Parmesan cheese, to serve

1. Melt half the butter in a large saucepan over medium-low heat. Add the onion, celery, and sage to the melted butter and cook for 3–4 minutes, until the onion is soft, stirring frequently. Stir in the flour and continue to cook for an additional 2 minutes.

2. Slowly add about one-quarter of the broth and stir well, scraping the bottom of the pan to mix in the flour. Pour in the remaining broth, stirring to combine, and bring to a boil.

3. Stir in the rice and season to taste with salt and pepper, if using. Reduce the heat and simmer gently, partly covered, for about 30 minutes, until the rice is just tender, stirring occasionally.

4. Meanwhile, melt the remaining butter in a large skillet over medium heat. Add the mushrooms and season to taste with salt and pepper, if using. Cook for about 8 minutes, until golden brown, stirring occasionally at first, then more often after they start to brown. Add the mushrooms to the soup.

5. Add the turkey to the soup and stir in the cream. Continue to simmer for about 10 minutes, until heated through. Taste and adjust the seasoning, if necessary. Ladle into warm serving bowls, garnish with sage, and serve with Parmesan cheese.

Christmas Turkey Salad

This salad provides a solution to the problem of all the little dishes of leftovers that make the refrigator crowded after the Christmas meal.

SERVES 4   PREP 10 MINS   COOK NONE

½ cup olive oil

¼ cup lemon juice

3 tablespoons cranberry sauce

1 tablespoon grainy mustard

leftover cooked vegetables, such as carrots, green beans, and/or broccoli (3–4 cups when prepared)

8 leftover roasted potatoes

2 (5-ounce) packages arugula

8 cooked turkey slices

⅔ cup Parmesan cheese shavings

1. Whisk together the oil, lemon juice, cranberry sauce, and mustard with a fork until combined.

2. Chop the cooked vegetables and roasted potatoes into bite-size pieces, put into a large bowl, add half the dressing, and toss until the vegetables are coated.

3. Divide the arugula among four serving plates. Pile the vegetables on top and arrange the turkey over the vegetables. Sprinkle the cheese shavings over the top and serve with the remaining dressing, adjusting the amount to taste.

Ham & Leek Risotto

The addition of leeks and peas makes this speedy risotto a satisfying family meal, and it is a perfect way of using up the Christmas ham.

SERVES 4   PREP 20 MINS   COOK 35 MINS

2 cups risotto rice

4 cups water

2 tablespoons olive oil

2 cups diced cooked ham

1 shallot, diced

2 leeks, white and light green parts only, trimmed and diced

¼ cup dry white wine

4 cups chicken broth, plus extra if needed

¼ cup finely chopped fresh parsley, plus extra to garnish

1 cup fresh or frozen peas

2 tablespoons butter

⅔ cup freshly grated Parmesan cheese, plus extra to garnish

salt and pepper (optional)

1. Put the rice into a large saucepan with the water and a generous pinch of salt, if using. Bring to a boil over high heat, then reduce the heat to low and simmer, uncovered, for 7 minutes. Drain the rice in a colander and set aside.

2. Heat the oil in the pan used to cook the rice. Add the ham, shallot, and leeks and cook, stirring, for about 3 minutes, until the vegetables begin to soften and the ham begins to brown. Add the wine and cook for an additional 1–2 minutes. Add the rice, broth, chopped parsley, and ¼–½ teaspoon of salt, if using, and bring to a boil. Reduce the heat to medium and simmer, stirring occasionally, for 12 minutes, or until most of the broth has evaporated.

3. Taste the risotto. If it is not yet cooked through, add a little more broth and cook for an additional few minutes. Stir in the peas in the last couple of minutes of cooking. Stir the butter and cheese into the risotto. Garnish with cheese and parsley and serve immediately.

Ham & Mushroom Quiche

Quiche is a tasty way of using up leftovers—it can be eaten hot or cold, so it is a good solution for those unstructured days after Christmas.

SERVES 4–6 .... PREP 30 MINS, PLUS 30 MINS' CHILLING .... COOK 45–50 MINS

1 tablespoon butter

1 small onion, finely chopped

2 cups sliced button mushrooms

1 cup diced cooked ham

2 eggs, beaten

1 cup light cream

½ cup shredded Gruyère or Swiss cheese

salt and pepper (optional)

PASTRY DOUGH

1⅔ cups all-purpose flour

1 stick butter

2–3 tablespoons cold water

1 talespoon flour, for dusting

1. To make the dough, sift the flour into a bowl and rub in the butter with your fingertips until the mixture resembles fine bread crumbs. Stir in just enough water to bind the mixture to a soft dough.

2. Roll out the dough on a lightly floured work surface and use to line a 9-inch tart pan. Press into the edges, trim the excess, and prick the bottom with a fork. Chill in the refrigerator for 15 minutes.

3. Preheat the oven to 400°F. Line the bottom with a piece of parchment paper and fill with pie weights or dried beans, then bake in the preheated oven for 10 minutes, until lightly browned. Remove from the oven and take out the paper and weights, then bake for an additional 10 minutes.

4. Melt the butter in a skillet, add the onion, and sauté for 2 minutes, then add the mushrooms and sauté, stirring, for an additional 2–3 minutes. Add the ham, then spread the mixture evenly in the pastry shell.

5. Put the eggs into a bowl with the cream and beat together, then season to taste with salt and pepper, if using. Pour into the pastry shell and sprinkle with the cheese. Bake for 20–25 minutes, until golden brown and just set.

Smoked Salmon Risotto

Smoked salmon is something usually eaten cold, but it also works well in hot dishes—and this tasty risotto makes a little go a long way.

SERVES 4	PREP 20 MINS	COOK 15–20 MINS

4 tablespoons unsalted butter

1 onion, finely chopped

½ small fennel bulb, finely chopped

2⅔ cups risotto rice

1¼ cups white wine

5 cups hot fish broth

1 (6-ounce) can smoked salmon, flaked

5 ounces smoked salmon, sliced into bite-size pieces

2 tablespoons fresh chervil or chopped flat-leaf parsley

salt and pepper (optional)

1. Melt half the butter in a large saucepan over medium heat, add the onion and fennel, and cook, stirring frequently, for 5–8 minutes, until transparent and soft. Add the rice and stir well to coat the grains in the butter. Cook, stirring, for 3 minutes, then add the wine, stir, and let simmer until most of the liquid has been absorbed.

2. With the broth simmering in a separate saucepan, add a ladleful to the rice and stir well. Cook, stirring constantly, until nearly all the liquid has been absorbed, then add another ladleful of broth. Continue to add the remaining broth in the same way until the rice is cooked but still firm to the bite and most or all of the broth has been added.

3. Remove from the heat and stir in the flaked and sliced smoked salmon and the remaining butter. Season to taste with salt and pepper, if using, sprinkle with the chervil, and serve immediately.

Salmon & Potato Casserole

If you have Brussels sprouts left over after Christmas dinner, this is a delicious way to use them with salmon fillets.

SERVES 4–6   *PREP 30 MINS*   *COOK 20 MINS*

1 tablespoon olive oil, for oiling

1 pound new potatoes

2 tablespoons olive oil

1 teaspoon salt

18 Brussels sprouts

½ teaspoon pepper

1½ pounds salmon fillet

2 tablespoons unsalted butter

1 tablespoon fresh dill

juice of 1 lemon

3 scallions

1. Preheat the oven to 450°F and oil a large baking dish. Slice the potatoes into thin circles and place them in the bottom of the dish in an even layer. Drizzle half the oil evenly over the potatoes, then sprinkle with half the salt. Place in the preheated oven.

2. Meanwhile, trim and thinly slice the sprouts. Put them into a medium bowl and toss with the remaining oil, half the remaining salt, and the pepper. Remove the dish from the oven and spread the sliced sprouts over the top of the potatoes in an even layer. Return to the oven. Cut the salmon into 2-inch chunks and season with the remaining salt. Put the butter into a small bowl and melt in the microwave. Finely chop the dill and add it to the butter with the lemon juice. Trim and slice the scallions.

3. Remove the dish from the oven and place the salmon pieces on top of the vegetables. Spoon the butter mixture over the salmon pieces and drizzle any remaining mixture over the vegetables. Sprinkle the scallions over the top. Return to the oven and bake for 10–12 minutes, until the salmon flakes easily with a fork and is cooked through. Serve immediately.

Green Bean Casserole

You can use of any leftover beans with this tasty casserole. Teamed with canned mushroom soup, this is a great standby after Christmas.

SERVES 4–6	PREP 10 MINS	COOK 40–45 MINS

5 cups 1½-inch green bean pieces

1¼ cups canned condensed mushroom soup

1 cup milk

1 teaspoon soy sauce

1 tablespoon vegetable oil

1 tablespoon butter

1 onion, sliced into rings

1. Preheat the oven to 350°F. Bring a saucepan of water to a boil and add the beans. Bring back to a boil and cook for 5 minutes. Drain well.

2. Put the soup, milk, and soy sauce into a bowl and mix together, then stir in the beans. Transfer to a 1½-quart casserole dish and distribute evenly. Bake in the preheated oven for 25–30 minutes, until bubbling and golden.

3. Meanwhile, heat the oil and butter in a skillet, add the onion rings, and cook over a fairly high heat, stirring frequently, until golden brown and crisp. Remove and drain on absorbent paper towels.

4. Arrange the onion rings on top of the casserole and bake for an additional 5 minutes. Serve hot.

1   2   2

Mushroom Stroganoff

A delicious vegetarian spin on the original beef stroganoff, this dish is quick to prepare and will use up any leftover mushrooms you may have.

SERVES 4	PREP 10 MINS	COOK 15–20 MINS

2 tablespoons butter

1 onion, finely chopped

7½ cups quartered button mushrooms (about 1 pound)

1 teaspoon tomato paste

1 teaspoon whole-grain mustard

⅔ cup crème fraîche

1 teaspoon paprika, plus extra to garnish

salt and pepper (optional)

fresh flat-leaf parsley sprigs, to garnish

1. Heat the butter in a large, heavy skillet. Add the onion and sauté gently for 5–10 minutes, until soft.

2. Add the mushrooms to the pan and sauté for a few minutes, until they begin to soften.

3. Stir in the tomato paste and mustard, then add the crème fraîche. Cook gently, stirring constantly, for 5 minutes.

4. Stir in the paprika and season with salt and pepper, if using, then garnish with parsley and serve immediately.

❄ Variation ❄

IF YOU PREFER TO BE COMPLETELY AUTHENTIC, YOU COULD USE THE MORE TRADITIONAL SOUR CREAM IN PLACE OF THE CRÈME FRAÎCHE.

1

2

3

From the Christmas Kitchen

* * * * * *

Indulgent Peppermint Hot Chocolate Mix

Peppermint crisp chocolate adds great flavor and a splash of color to a classic festive treat—make a batch and give as a gift.

MAKES 6	PREP 10 MINS	COOK NONE

10 cups instant dry milk (about 1½ pounds)

1½ cups unsweetened cocoa powder

1½ cups sugar

8 ounces peppermint crisp chocolate, chopped

1. You will need six sterilized 16-ounce, wide-mouth canning jars for this recipe. To prepare the gift jars, divide all of the ingredients evenly among the jars. Add the ingredients in layers, starting with the dried milk. Place the lids on the jars and secure tightly.

2. Attach a tag to each jar with these directions:

How to prepare Indulgent Peppermint Hot Chocolate
Pour the contents of the jar into a medium bowl and mix to combine. For each serving, put 3 tablepoons of the mixture into a mug and add ¾ cup of hot water or milk. Stir until the mix is completely dissolved. Serve immediately.

Tip

THE HOT CHOCOLATE MIX WILL KEEP FOR UP TO SIX MONTHS, IF COVERED TIGHTLY AND STORED IN A COOL, DRY PLACE.

Whiskey Fudge

If you know of any chocolate- and whiskey-lovers, then this is the perfect treat for them. You can use a brandy instead of whiskey, if you prefer.

SERVES 16   PREP 15 MINS   COOK 10–15 MINS, PLUS SETTING

1 tablespoon sunflower oil,
for oiling

1 cup firmly packed
light brown sugar

1 stick unsalted butter, diced

1 (14-ounce) can sweetened
condensed milk

2 tablespoons light corn syrup

6 ounces semisweet chocolate,
coarsely chopped

¼ cup whiskey

¼ cup walnut pieces

1. Lightly brush an 8-inch square baking pan with oil. Line it with nonstick parchment paper, snipping diagonally into the corners, then pressing the paper into the pan so that the bottom and sides are lined.

2. Put the sugar, butter, condensed milk, and corn syrup into a heavy saucepan. Heat gently, stirring, until the sugar has dissolved.

3. Increase the heat, bring to the mixture to a boil, and boil for 12–15 minutes, or until the mixture reaches 240°F on a candy thermometer. (If you don't have a candy thermometer, spoon a little of the syrup into some ice water; it will form a soft ball when it is ready.) As the temperature rises, stir the fudge occasionally so the sugar doesn't stick and burn. Remove the fudge from the heat. Add the chocolate and whiskey and stir together until the chocolate has melted and the mixture is smooth.

4. Preheat the broiler to medium-hot. Put the walnuts on a baking sheet and toast them under the broiler for 2–3 minutes, or until browned. Coarsely chop them.

5. Pour the mixture into the prepared baking pan, smooth the surface using a spatula, and sprinkle with the walnuts. Let cool for 1 hour. Cover with plastic wrap, then chill in the refrigerator for 1–2 hours, or until firm. Lift the fudge out of the pan, peel off the paper, and cut into small squares. Store in an airtight container in a cool, dry place for up to two weeks.

Espresso Truffles

The delicate, edible gold leaf on these tasty truffles makes them an extra special gift for any chocoholic.

SERVES 12   PREP 40 MINS   COOK 5–10 MINS, PLUS SETTING

10 ounces semisweet chocolate, coarsely chopped

2 tablespoons heavy cream

1 tablespoon strong espresso coffee, cooled

2 tablespoons coffee liqueur

4 tablespoons unsalted butter, softened and diced

edible gold leaf, to decorate (optional)

1. Put 4 ounces of the chocolate and all the cream into a heatproof bowl set over a saucepan of gently simmering water and heat, stirring, until the chocolate has melted.

2. Remove from the heat, add the coffee, coffee liqueur, and butter and whisk for 3–4 minutes, or until thickened. Transfer to an airtight container and chill in the refrigerator for 6–8 hours, or until firm.

3. Line a baking sheet with nonstick parchment paper. Scoop out teaspoons of the mixture and roll them into truffle-size balls. Place the balls on the prepared baking sheet, cover with plastic wrap, and freeze for 6–8 hours.

4. Put the remaining chocolate into a heatproof bowl set over a saucepan of gently simmering water and heat until melted. Using two forks, dip each truffle into the chocolate to coat evenly. Return to the prepared sheet and chill in the refrigerator for 1–2 hours, or until firm. Top each truffle with edible gold leaf to decorate, if using. Store in an airtight container in the refrigerator for up to five days.

Pistachio & Apricot Nougat

Delicious homemade nougat, with pistachios and dried apricots, is the perfect gift for anyone with a sweet tooth.

| SERVES 16 | PREP 30 MINS, PLUS SETTING | COOK 15 MINS |

edible rice paper
1¼ cups superfine sugar
½ cup light corn syrup
⅓ cup honey
2 tablespoons water
pinch of salt
1 egg white
½ teaspoon vanilla extract
4 tablespoons unsalted butter, softened and diced
⅓ cup coarsely chopped pistachio nuts
⅓ cup finely chopped dried apricots

1. Line a 7-inch square loose-bottom cake pan with plastic wrap, leaving an overhang. Line the bottom with a piece of the rice paper.

2. Put the sugar, corn syrup, honey, water, and salt into a heavy saucepan. Heat gently until the sugar has dissolved, tilting the pan to mix the ingredients together. Increase the heat, bring to a boil, and boil for 8 minutes, or until the mixture reaches 250°F on a candy thermometer.

3. Whisk the egg white in a clean, greasefree bowl until firm. Gradually pour in one-quarter of the hot syrup in a thin stream while still beating the egg. Continue beating for 5 minutes, until the mixture is stiff enough to hold its shape on the beaters.

4. Put the saucepan containing the remaining syrup over low heat for 2 minutes, or until the mixture reaches 290°F on a candy thermometer. Gradually pour the syrup over the egg mixture while beating.

5. Add the vanilla extract and butter and beat for an additional 5 minutes. Add the pistachio nuts and apricots and stir.

6. Pour the mixture into the pan and level with a spatula. Cover with rice paper and chill in the refrigerator for 8–10 hours, or until fairly firm.

7. Lift the nougat out of the pan and cut into 16 squares. Store in an airtight container in the refrigerator for up to five days.

Double Chocolate Brownie Mix

This beats a packaged brownie mix any day. It makes a great gift, one that takes away most of the work and leaves all of the pleasure.

MAKES 6   PREP 10 MINS   COOK NONE

6 cups all-purpose flour

1½ teaspoons salt

2¾ cups firmly packed light brown sugar

4 cups granulated sugar

4 cups unsweetened cocoa powder

4 cups toasted hazelnuts, chopped

3 cups mini semisweet chocolate chips

1. You will need six sterilized 16-ounce, wide-mouth canning jars for this recipe. To prepare the gift jars, divide all of the ingredients evenly among the jars. Add the ingredients in layers, starting with the flour. Place the lids on the jars and secure tightly.

2. Attach a gift tag to each jar with these directions:

How to prepare Double Chocolate Brownies

You will need:

2 extra-large eggs

2 tablespoons milk

1 teaspoon vanilla extract

1 stick butter, melted, plus extra for greasing

Preheat the oven to 350°F and grease a 9 x 13-inch rectangular cake pan.

Transfer the brownie mix from the jar to a large mixing bowl. Put the eggs, milk, and vanilla extract into a separate bowl and mix to combine. Add the egg mixture to the dry ingredients and mix until well combined. Stir in the melted butter and mix to combine.

Transfer the batter to the prepared pan and bake in the preheated oven for about 20 minutes, until the top is dry and a toothpick inserted into the center comes out almost clean. Place the pan on a wire rack and let cool completely. Serve at room temperature.

Christmas Ginger Thins

These spicy ginger thins will not only tickle your recipients' taste buds, but will fill their homes with the festive aroma of freshly baked cookies.

MAKES 72	PREP 30 MINS. PLUS FREEZING	COOK NONE

4 cups all-purpose flour

2 teaspoons baking soda

1 teaspoon salt

2 tablespoons ground ginger

2 teaspoons ground cinnamon

1 teaspoon ground cloves

3 sticks unsalted butter, at room temperature

1 cup granulated sugar

1 cup firmly packed dark brown sugar

2 extra-large eggs

¾ cup molasses

2 cups raw brown sugar

1. You will need six sterilized 16-ounce, wide-mouth canning jars for this recipe. Line two large baking sheets with parchment paper.

2. Put the flour, baking soda, salt, ginger, cinnamon, and cloves into a medium bowl and mix to combine.

3. Put the butter, granulated sugar, and dark brown sugar into a large bowl and beat until light and fluffy. Add the eggs and molasses and mix until incorporated. Add the flour mixture and beat until incorporated, scraping down the side of the bowl once or twice.

4. Put the raw brown sugar into a shallow bowl. Shape the dough into 1½-inch balls and roll in the sugar to coat completely. Place the balls on the prepared baking sheet spaced well apart. When the first sheet is full, use your fingertips to flatten the balls into circles about 3 inches in diameter (they should be about the same diameter as the canning jars) and ⅛ inch thick. If your fingers become too sticky, dip them in the sugar. Place the sheet in the freezer. Continue to shape the remaining dough until all the dough has been used and both sheets are full. Place the second sheet in the freezer and freeze for at least 4 hours or overnight, until the cookies are completely frozen.

5. Stack 12 frozen cookies in each of the six jars. Attach a gift tag to each jar with these directions:

How to bake Christmas Ginger Thins

Keep frozen until required. Preheat the oven to 350°F and place the cookies on an ungreased baking sheet. Bake in the preheated oven for 12–14 minutes, until the cookies are dry on the top and beginning to crisp. Remove from the oven and transfer to a wire rack to cool completely. Serve at room temperature.

Vanilla Fudge

With just a few simple ingredients and you can make the creamiest vanilla fudge ever, perfect for a Christmas treat.

MAKES 16   PREP 15 MINS, PLUS SETTING   COOK 15–20 MINS

1 tablespoon sunflower oil,
for oiling

2¼ cups superfine sugar

6 tablespoons unsalted butter

⅔ cup milk

⅔ cup canned evaporated milk

2 teaspoons vanilla extract

1. Lightly brush an 8-inch square baking pan with oil. Line it with nonstick parchment paper, snipping diagonally into the corners, then pressing the paper into the pan so that the base and sides are lined.

2. Put the sugar, butter, milk, and evaporated milk into a heavy saucepan. Heat gently, stirring, until the sugar has dissolved.

3. Increase the heat, bring the mixture to a boil, and boil for 12–15 minutes, or until it reaches 240°F on a candy thermometer. (If you don't have a candy thermometer, spoon a little of the syrup into some iced water; it will form a soft ball when it is ready.) As the temperature rises, stir the fudge occasionally so the sugar doesn't stick and burn.

4. Remove the pan from the heat, add the vanilla extract, and beat with a wooden spoon until thickened.

5. Pour the mixture into the prepared pan and smooth the surface with a spatula. Let cool for 1 hour, until set.

6. Lift the fudge out of the pan, peel off the paper, and cut into small squares. Store in an airtight container in a cool, dry place for up to two weeks.

Nutly Peppermint Bark

Kids and adults alike will love this treat. If you can't get hold of peppermint candy canes, substitute them with any hard mint candies.

MAKES 25   PREP 20 MINS, PLUS CHILLING   COOK 3-4 MINS

6 ounces red-and-white striped peppermint candy canes, broken into pieces

1 pound white chocolate, coarsely chopped

1 cup chopped mixed nuts

1. Line a 12 x 8-inch rectangular baking pan with nonstick parchment paper.

2. Put the broken candy canes into a large plastic food bag and seal tightly. Using a rolling pin, bang the bag until the canes are crushed into small pieces.

3. Put the chocolate into a heatproof bowl set over a saucepan of gently simmering water and heat until melted. Remove from the heat and stir in three-quarters of the crushed candy canes.

4. Pour the mixture into the prepared pan, smooth the surface, using a spatula, and sprinkle with the chopped nuts and remaining candy. Press down slightly to make sure they stick. Cover with plastic wrap and chill in the refrigerator for 30 minutes, or until firm.

5. Break the peppermint bark into small, uneven pieces. Store in an airtight container in a cool, dry place for up to two weeks.

Mixed Nuts in Herbed Salt

Simple to make and wonderfully tasty, these addictive pan-roasted nuts are bursting with protein, healthy fats, and plenty of flavor.

SERVES 4	PREP 10 MINS, PLUS COOLING	COOK 5 MINS

1 tablespoon olive oil

2 fresh rosemary sprigs, leaves torn from the stems

½ cup cashew nuts

½ cup pecans

½ cup unblanched almonds

½ cup unblanched hazelnuts

½ teaspoon sea salt

1. Heat the oil and rosemary in a skillet, then swirl the oil around the pan to flavor it with the rosemary. Add the nuts and cook for 2–3 minutes, until lightly toasted.

2. Stir in the salt, then spoon the nuts into a bowl and let cool. Any leftover nuts can be stored in the refrigerator in a plastic container or canning jar for up to three days.

❄ Variation ❄

TRY REPLACING THE ROSEMARY WITH A LITTLE CURRY POWDER OR A BLEND OF GROUND TURMERIC, GARAM MASALA, SMOKED PAPRIKA, AND A PINCH OF CHILI POWDER.

Corn Relish

This golden relish will be a popular Christmas gift—it can be served with roasted meat or salad and it has a long refrigerator life.

MAKES 1 LB 5 OZ	PREP 10 MINS, PLUS COOLING	COOK 30 MINS

5 fresh ears of corn (about 2 pounds), shucked

1 red bell pepper, seeded and finely diced

2 celery stalks, finely chopped

1 red onion, finely chopped

⅔ cup sugar

1 tablespoon salt

2 tablespoons dry mustard

½ teaspoon celery seeds

small pinch of turmeric (optional)

1 cup apple cider vinegar

½ cup water

1. Bring a large saucepan of water to a boil and fill a bowl with ice water. Add the corn to the boiling water, bring back to a boil, and cook for 2 minutes, or until the kernels are tender-crisp. Using tongs, immediately plunge the cobs into the cold water to halt cooking. Remove from the water and cut the kernels from the cobs, then set aside.

2. Add the red bell pepper, celery, and onion to the corn cooking water, bring back to a boil, and boil for 2 minutes, or until tender-crisp. Drain well and return to the pan with the corn kernels.

3. Put the sugar, salt, mustard, celery seeds, and turmeric, if using, into a bowl and mix together, then stir in the vinegar and water. Add to the pan, bring the liquid to a boil, then reduce the heat and simmer for 15 minutes, stirring occasionally.

4. Ladle the relish into hot, sterilized canning jars, filling them to within ½ inch of the top of each jar. Wipe the rims and secure the lids. Let the relish cool completely, then refrigerate for up to two months.

Christmas Crafts

* * * * * *

Handmade Stocking

Fill this cute little Christmas stocking with gifts and it will look perfect hanging by the fireplace. It requires simple sewing skills.

⤜⤏❦⤍⤛

two 10 x 12-inch pieces of ⅛-inch-thick, pressed 100-percent wool felt

contrasting cotton fabric scraps

matching or coordinating embroidery thread

YOU WILL ALSO NEED

a large piece of paper, pair of scissors, pins, sharp pair of fabric scissors, pinking shears, darning needle

1. Enlarge the Christmas Stocking and Christmas Tree for Stocking templates on page 221 to the required size, using a photocopier. The finished stocking for this project is 11 inches in height, but you can vary the size. Copy and cut out the following templates: two stocking shapes and one Christmas tree.

2. Make the following templates using a large piece of paper: two rectangular cuff shapes, measuring 9 inches long by 4 inches wide, and one rectangular loop shape, measuring 12 inches long by 2½ inches wide.

3. Pin the stocking template to the felt fabric and cut out, using the pair of fabric scissors. Because the felt fabric is the same on both sides, there is no need to worry about turning the template over.

4. Pin the cuff templates, tree, and loop to the contrasting cotton fabric and cut out, using the pinking shears.

5. Thread the darning needle with a length of embroidery thread and tie a knot in the end. Use the same embroidery thread for all of the sewing.

6. Place the Christmas tree shape on top of one of the felt stocking shapes, so that the foot of the stocking is facing left and the pattern of the Christmas tree is the right way around. Secure the thread to the back of the stocking shape and sew the Christmas tree on top of the felt, using a simple running stitch.

7. The cuff template is much bigger than the width of the stocking so the edges of the cuff can be folded around the top of the stocking. Place the felt stocking shape, Christmas tree showing, on top of the inside of the cuff shape. Fold half of the fabric over the top of the stocking, making sure that the material is the right way around if there is a pattern. Fold the edges of the cuff to the inside of the stocking and, using a simple running stitch, sew each edge of the cuff to the stocking along the sides. Leave the pinking shear edge unattached at the front.

8. Place both pieces of the stocking together. Use a simple running stitch to sew around the edges of the stocking, leaving the top cuffed edge open.

9. Fold the loop shape in half lengthwise, making sure that the pattern is on the outside, and sew along the length using running stitch. Leave the pinked edge showing. Form a loop and place each end inside the stocking at the top right-hand side of the cuff. Sew each end of the loop to the inside of the stocking, using running stitch. Check all pins have been removed before hanging up for Christmas.

Decorative Jars

These tealight holders cast a festive shadow of snowflakes. Vary the size of the jars and the color of the snowflakes to create a magical atmosphere.

assorted glass jars in various shapes and sizes

small snowflake-shaped paper punch

white tissue paper

craft glue

crochet snowflakes

assorted festive ribbons, twine, and/or fabric, cut to 20 inches long

battery-operated tealights

YOU WILL ALSO NEED

glue spreader or stiff paintbrush

1. Wash the glass jars in mild soapy water to make sure they are free of grease.

2. Using a snowflake-shape paper punch, stamp out a selection of tissue paper snowflakes. Use a glue spreader or stiff paintbrush to apply glue to the entire surface of one of the jars. Place the tissue paper snowflakes on the layer of glue in a random pattern. Apply a layer of glue over the top of them. Set the jar aside to dry—don't worry if the jar looks white, because the craft glue will dry clear.

3. Cover one side of a crochet snowflake with a generous coating of glue and attach it to another jar. Choose either two larger crochet snowflakes or a selection of smaller crochet snowflakes to attach to more jars in a random pattern.

4. Let the finished jars dry for about 3 hours.

5. When the jars are completely dry, tie a selection of ribbons around the neck of each jar, turn on the tealights, and place inside.

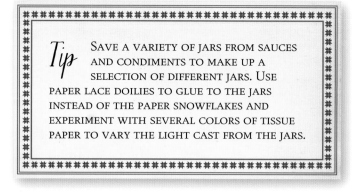

Tip SAVE A VARIETY OF JARS FROM SAUCES AND CONDIMENTS TO MAKE UP A SELECTION OF DIFFERENT JARS. USE PAPER LACE DOILIES TO GLUE TO THE JARS INSTEAD OF THE PAPER SNOWFLAKES AND EXPERIMENT WITH SEVERAL COLORS OF TISSUE PAPER TO VARY THE LIGHT CAST FROM THE JARS.

207

Angel Tree Decoration

This delightful card stock design incorporates a balsa wood angel that can be removed from the card to hang on the Christmas tree.

300-gsm white card stock

gold paper

small and large-weave burlap

scrap card stock

1/16-inch-thick board

1/8-inch-thick balsa wood

white and cadmium yellow acrylic paints

gold enamel paint

thin craft wire

YOU WILL ALSO NEED

craft knife, ruler, cutting mat, pencil, scoring tool, double-sided tape, black felt-tip pen, paintbrush, long-nose pliers, superglue, pin

1. Using a craft knife and ruler on a cutting mat, cut a piece of the white card stock to 6⅛ x 7½ inches. Score down the center with a scoring tool and fold in half. Attach the gold paper to the front of the folded card with double-sided tape. Trim with the craft knife and ruler. Cut a 6⅛ x 3¾-inch piece of small-weave burlap. Use an existing frayed edge for the right-hand edge, or fray it by pulling a few vertical strands away. Attach the burlap with double-sided tape so that it fits exactly over the gold paper.

2. Enlarge the templates on page 221 on a photocopier as directed and cut out. Draw around the templates on scrap card stock and cut out with a craft knife and ruler on a cutting mat.

3. Draw around the angel silhouette onto the large-weave burlap with the black felt-tip pen and cut out. Attach to the card stock with double-sided tape.

4. Using the template, cut a large heart from gold paper and attach it to a piece of board with double-sided tape, then attach to the burlap angel. Open the card and lay flat, then cut a small, upside-down "V" in the top edge of the card front. This will serve as a hook for the balsa wood angel.

5. Using the templates and craft knife, cut the wings, angel body, and a small heart from balsa wood. Paint the head and wings with white acrylic paint. Add a tiny amount of yellow to the white to make a cream for the dress. While drying, paint the heart with gold enamel paint. Cut a 5-inch length of wire with the pair of pliers and twist the ends together for a length of ½ inch, forming a hoop for the halo.

6. Paint white polka dots on the dress. When dry, superglue the angel body to the wings and the heart to the body. Use the pin to make a hole at the top of the wings behind the angel's back. Superglue the twisted wire of the halo into the hole.

Christmas Snowflake Card

Just one template can be used to create four classy card designs that will look stunning displayed in the home.

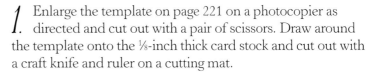

⅛-inch thick card stock

300-gsm slightly textured watercolor paper

300-gsm white card stock

silver and/or gold spray-paint

silver and/or gold card stock

You will also need

pair of scissors, pencil, craft knife, ruler, cutting mat, masking tape, bone folder, double-sided tape, old newspaper, dust mask, and protective gloves

1. Enlarge the template on page 221 on a photocopier as directed and cut out with a pair of scissors. Draw around the template onto the ⅛-inch thick card stock and cut out with a craft knife and ruler on a cutting mat.

2. Place the template on the watercolor paper and secure with masking tape. Make sure there is enough space to create a 6-inch square. Turn the paper over and rub firmly all over the template area with a bone folder to create an impression.

3. Remove the template. Make sure that the embossed snowflake is in the center of the paper, then trim to 6 inches square.

4. Cut a 6 x 12-inch piece of white card stock. Score down the center with a bone folder and fold in half. Use double-sided tape around the edges of the embossed snowflake panel to attach it to the card.

5. Repeat steps 2 to 4 to create a second card, but attach the watercolor paper to the opposite side of the white card to create a reversed impression.

6. To make a third card, place the template on the front of folded white card (see step 4). Protect your work surface with old newspaper. Wearing a dust mask and protective gloves, spray silver and/or gold paint over the card. When dry, remove the template to reveal the snowflake.

7. To make a fourth card, cut a 6 x 12-inch piece of silver or gold card stock. Score down the center with a bone folder and fold in half. Respray the snowflake template so that it contrasts with the card, if needed, and attach it to the card front with double-sided tape.

Christmas Wreath

You won't need special floristry skills to create this simple indoor decoration. Vary the patterns, colors, and ribbons for different occasions.

20 yards assorted ribbons of various widths with a Christmas theme

10 yards of 1-inch-wide natural jute burlap ribbon

10-inch round, flat wire wreath frame

YOU WILL ALSO NEED

pair of fabric scissors, ruler or tape measure

1. Cut various lengths between 10 and 14 inches from the assorted and jute burlap ribbons, using a ruler or tape measure as a guide. Don't worry about being too precise—this design looks more effective with materials of various lengths.

2. Tie the first piece of ribbon in a bow around the wire frame. The aim is to fill the entire frame with ribbon bows, so start anywhere with the first one. Again, don't worry about being too neat—the aim is for a rustic, shabby-chic look.

3. Use different lengths, colors, and patterns of ribbon and continue to tie bows all the way around the frame, alternating between the jute burlap and other ribbons as you progress. Gently push each bow toward the previous bow to make sure there isn't any of the wire frame visible.

4. Once you fill the entire frame, tie a final length of ribbon around the frame to create a loop for hanging the wreath. The wreath works both ways when you hang it, so turn it around for two styles in one.

❄ *Tip* ❄

THE SIZE OF THE WREATH IS ADAPTABLE. SIMPLY BUY A SMALLER OR LARGER FLAT WIRE WREATH FRAME AND ADJUST THE QUANTITY OF RIBBON OR FABRIC. PURCHASE FRAMES FROM A LOCAL FLORIST OR ONLINE.

Gift Tags & Gift Decorations

Add a touch of vintage chic to your Christmas presents with these elegant gift tags. You can vary the lacy design with a variety of paper doilies.

medium-weight brown kraft card stock

paper doilies with a scalloped edge

hole punch reinforcement labels (optional)

thin silver ribbon or twine, 6–8 inches long

YOU WILL ALSO NEED

paper, pair of scissors, pencil, hole punch, glue stick

1. Create templates on paper to your chosen size and cut out. Rectangles about 3½ inches long by 2½ inches wide and circles 2½ inches in diameter work well for this.

2. Draw around the template onto the brown kraft card stock and cut out with a pair of scissors.

3. Punch a hole in the top of the gift tag. Apply a layer of glue to the bottom half of the tag with the glue stick.

4. Place one of the lace edges of a paper doily onto the layer of glue on the bottom half of the tag. Choose a symmetrical section of the doily so the scalloped edge becomes a feature of the tag. Trim the doily around the edges of the gift tag.

5. Apply the hole reinforcers, if using. Thread a length of ribbon or twine through the hole and knot it to create a tie for your tag.

Tip VARY THE COLOR OF THE CARD STOCK TO CREATE A VARIETY OF GIFT TAGS TO COMPLEMENT YOUR WRAPPING PAPER.

Christmas Card Tree Decorations

If you'd like to give something more than a card, but you are not sure of what to buy, this smart card doubles as a stylish tree decoration.

❧

300-gsm brown card stock

pale green plain paper

brown glitter card stock

brown corrugated cardboard

¼-inch-wide red ribbon,
3¼ inches long

pale green handmade paper

¹⁄₁₆-inch-wide green ribbon,
4½ inches long

small deep red glass bead

YOU WILL ALSO NEED

*pencil, craft knife, ruler,
cutting mat, scoring tool,
hole punch, glue stick,
double-sided tape*

1. Enlarge the template on page 220 on a photocopier to the required size and cut out. Draw around the template on the brown card stock and cut out with a craft knife and ruler on a cutting mat. Score down the center with a scoring tool and fold. Punch a hole near the top.

2. Cover the inside of the tree with glue stick. Stick the plain green paper on one half of the inside, placing it down the center fold and making sure it adheres well. Trim with the craft knife. Repeat on the opposite side. Cut out the punched hole with the craft knife.

3. Cut a trunk from brown glitter card stock and attach in two pieces to the front and back of the card with double-sided tape. Cut the container from brown corrugated cardboard and attach in the same way.

4. Attach the red ribbon with double-sided tape, running it over the spine of the card.

5. Use a glue stick to adhere the green handmade-quality paper in one piece to the front and back of the outside of the card. Cut out the punched hole. Create a loop for hanging from the green ribbon, threading the deep red glass bead onto it before tying it off.

Decorative Centerpiece

Bring some sparkle to your festive feast with this special table centerpiece.
Have fun collecting old buttons and vintage ribbon for this project.

old newspaper

pinecones in a variety of
shapes and sizes

snow spray

glass cookie jar

mini LED battery-operated
lights

20–30 gold sequins

1 yard jute burlap ribbon,
at least ½ inch thick

YOU WILL ALSO NEED

protective mask and gloves,
craft glue

1. In a well-ventilated room, lay the newspaper on a flat surface and spread out the pinecones. Using a protective mask and gloves, spray the pinecones with the snow spray, turning the cones around to make sure that all parts are covered with a light coating. Let dry for about 30 minutes.

2. Once the cones are dry, place an initial selection of cones in the bottom of the glass cookie jar. Twist the first section of the LED mini lights around the pinecones and start adding more cones to the jar, twisting the lights around them as you fill the jar. When you get to the top of the jar, carefully disguise the battery section of the LED lights in the middle of the pinecones, making sure you can still access it to turn them on.

3. Stick sequins to the ends of the jute burlap ribbon in a random pattern, using blobs of craft glue. Once the glue has completely dried and the sequins are securely attached, place the ribbon around the top of the jar and tie in a bow.

4. Turn the lights on and replace the lid of the cookie jar.

Country-Style Garland

Perfect for creating a cozy, in-the-country mood, this will bring festive cheer to your home. Make short ones or a few longer ones.

small-weave burlap fabric,
12 inches square

large-weave burlap fabric,
12 inches square

scraps of pale green and
deep red felt

scraps of deep red gingham
and plain red cotton fabric

natural twine

decorative gold fine thread

5 red buttons,
¾ inch in diameter

embroidery needle

deep red embroidery thread

thin craft wire

6 tiny wooden clothespins

2 tiny felt hearts

YOU WILL ALSO NEED

pair of scissors, tailor's
chalk, craft knife,
cutting mat, tape
measure, fabric glue,
pair of long-nose pliers,
strong double-sided tape

1. Enlarge the templates on page 220 on a photocopier as directed and cut out using scissors. Using tailor's chalk and either a pair of scissors or a craft knife on a cutting mat, cut out the following: two circles from small-weave burlap, two from large-weave burlap; two large stars from each burlap, one small star from green felt; four angel bodies from large-weave burlap; four angel wings from small-weave burlap; two large hearts from red gingham, two from red felt; two small hearts from red gingham, two from red felt, two from green felt.

2. Lay a 1½-yard length of twine on a work surface and twist the gold thread around it. Tie a loop at each end and fray the ends.

3. Cover one side of the buttons with fabric glue and attach the red felt. Cut around the buttons with a craft knife. Pass the needle and thread through the buttonholes once so the thread ends dangle from the back of the button by about ⅝ inch. Make sure that two of the buttons have extra thread hanging.

4. Arrange the embellishments on the string, working out from the center. Run a length of thin wire around the top of the red and gingham large hearts with a pair of pliers and use double-sided tape to sandwich between the fabrics. Glue a small green heart to the plain red side and add one of the buttons. Use two clothespins to attach the string.

5. Construct the angels in the same way, but simply sandwich the string in between the head and tops of the wings. Sandwich the wings (two sets per angel) in between the bodies. Glue the tiny felt hearts in place.

6. Construct the remaining embellishments in the same way, using wire to strengthen them, then attach them to the string.

Advent Calendar

Every child knows that the Advent calendar means Christmas isn't too far away. Choose your own treats to fill this delightful calendar.

beige thick cotton fabric
1 yard square

red and dark green felt

roll of laminating film

2 dowels, 14¼ inches long

bright red, soft thick fabric
25 x 37 inches

sewing needle and deep red
strong cotton thread

extra-strong iron-on
stitch witchery
(hemming tape)

6 pairs of deep red baby
socks, for 0–3 months old

6 pairs of deep green baby
socks, for 0–3 months old

25 Christmas tree
embellishments in red,
green, and gold

24 tiny wooden clothespins

1½ yards of ½-inch-wide
green ribbon

large silver bell

¼-inch-wide red ribbon,
14¼ inches long

YOU WILL ALSO NEED

*pair of scissors, craft knife,
ruler, cutting mat, pinking
shears, straight pins,
basting thread, strong
double-sided tape, steam
iron, fabric glue*

1. Enlarge the box templates on page 221 on a photocopier as directed and cut out using scissors. Cut 24 large rectangles from the beige fabric, using a craft knife and a ruler on a cutting mat. Cut 24 small squares from red felt with pinking shears.

2. Use the template to cut the tree from green felt, place on the beige fabric, and cut out a slightly larger tree for a border. Laminate the sheet of numbers, then cut out with the craft knife and ruler.

3. Place one dowel at the top of the large piece of red fabric and fold the top edge of the fabric over. Pin, then baste the hem. Sew by hand with red thread, then remove the basting stitches. Repeat at the bottom of the fabric.

4. Temporarily position all the beige squares and the beige tree on the red fabric with double-sided tape, making sure that they are evenly positioned. Using the iron-on stitch witchery around the edges and following the manufacturer's directions, attach them to the red fabric, one row at a time.

5. Using fabric glue, adhere the red felt squares about halfway up and ¼ inch in from the right-hand side. Use double-sided tape to attach the numbers, centered, to each red square. Attach the green felt tree to the beige tree with fabric glue. Sew the socks to the tops of corners of the beige squares. Open them completely to add your treats, then stick the heels down with fabric glue. Use fabric glue to attach the tree embellishments, making sure sock number 24 has two slightly overlapping trees. Add the clothespins to look like they are holding the socks up. Tie bows in the green ribbon, attach the bell, and sew to the tree in the bottom right-hand corner.

6. To create hanging loops, use the craft knife to make two horizontal incisions just below the dowel, wide enough to thread the red ribbon through and under the dowel. Slightly overlap the ribbon and sew together. Move the ribbon around to hide the sewn part behind the dowel. Check all pins have been removed before hanging up for Christmas.

Templates

Country-Style
Garland (enlarge by 200%)

Christmas Card Tree
Decoration
(enlarge by 200%)

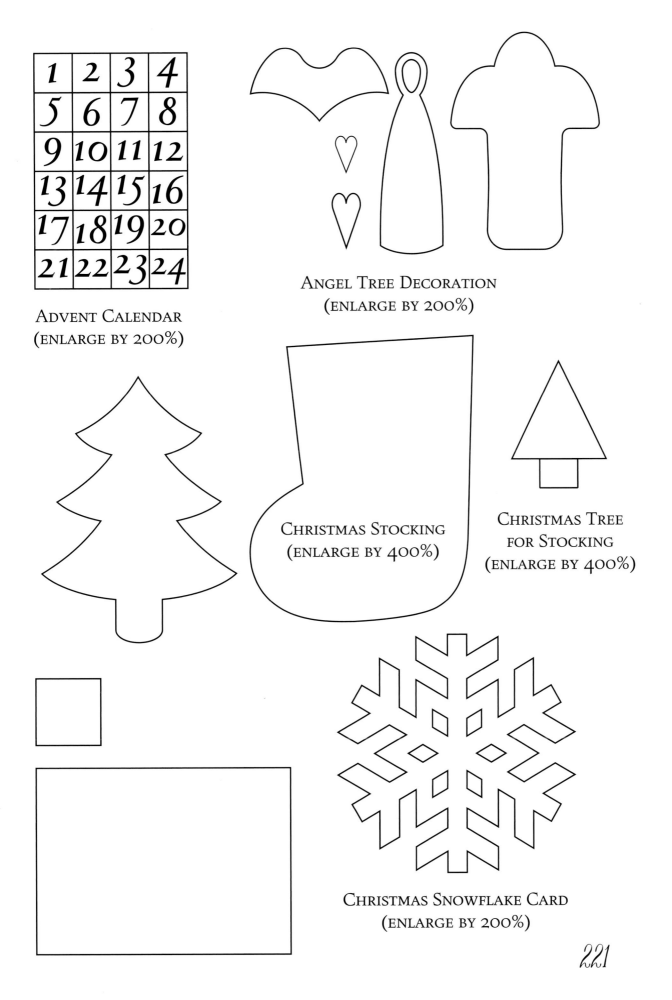

1	2	3	4
5	6	7	8
9	10	11	12
13	14	15	16
17	18	19	20
21	22	23	24

ADVENT CALENDAR
(ENLARGE BY 200%)

ANGEL TREE DECORATION
(ENLARGE BY 200%)

CHRISTMAS STOCKING
(ENLARGE BY 400%)

CHRISTMAS TREE
FOR STOCKING
(ENLARGE BY 400%)

CHRISTMAS SNOWFLAKE CARD
(ENLARGE BY 200%)

Index

DEC 2 1 2015